One
With All the Earth

SHRINE OF THE BAB ON MOUNT CARMEL, HAIFA, ISRAEL

ONE
With All the Earth

An Introduction to the Baha'i Teachings

by Janice Mazidi

Kalimát Press
Los Angeles

Copyright © 2003 by Kalimát Press
All Rights Reserved
Manufactured in the United States of America

Library of Congress Cataloging-in-Publication Data

Mazidi, Janice, 1958-
One with all the earth :
an introduction to the Baha'i teachings
/ by Janice Mazidi.
p. cm.
Includes bibliographical references.
ISBN 1-890688-30-4 (pbk.)
1. Bahai Faith--Doctrines.
2. Baha'u'llah, 1817-1892. I. Title.
BP365.M35 2003
297.9'3--dc21   2003006912

Kalimát Press
1600 Sawtelle Boulevard
Suite 310
Los Angeles, California 90025

www.kalimat.com
kalimatp@aol.com

Contents

Preface

Part One: **The Story of Baha'u'llah**

  1 ~ First Light: The Dawn of a New Age   *3*
  2 ~ Banished: Exile to Baghdad   *15*
  3 ~ Solitude: In Kurdistan   *23*
  4 ~ Paradise: The Garden of Ridvan   *31*
  5 ~ Final Exile: The Most Desolate of Cities   *41*
  6 ~ The Country: A Devotion Kings Might Envy   *55*
  7 ~ Final Passage: A Vision for the Ages   *65*

Part Two: **Baha'i Principles**

  8 ~ Transition and Succession   *71*
  9 ~ Social Principles   *75*

Part Three: **The Teachings of Baha'u'llah**

  10 ~ Our Spiritual Reality   *89*
  11 ~ Spiritual Virtues   *93*
  12 ~ The True Seeker   *107*
  13 ~ Your Spiritual Path   *115*

References   *119*
Suggested Reading   *125*
    Websites   *126*

SOME BAHA'IS IN LOS ANGELES, CALIFORNIA

Preface

WHAT IS THE BAHA'I FAITH? Where did it come from? Who are the Baha'is? What do they believe?

On one level, the answers to these questions are simple and uncomplicated. But the most simple truths are often the most profound. The Baha'i teachings can be summarized in three ideas:

• ***The Unity of God:*** Baha'is believe that there is only one God—even though the followers of various religions call him by different names. All of the peoples of the world worship the same God, who is infinite and unknowable.

• ***The Unity of Humanity:*** This is another simple idea. Baha'is believe that all people are one.

But this idea is, perhaps, the most deep and difficult of all Baha'i teachings, since it involves the need for a new human identity. All the old barriers that have divided people from one another, all lesser identities of race, culture, language, nationality, caste, rank, class, gender, religion, and so forth, must now be set aside in the larger quest for unity among all people.

The principle of the oneness of humanity is the pivot around which all the Baha'i teachings revolve. It is no mere expression of sentiment, nor is it just a pious hope for a happy future. Its implications are deeper. They demand that we, actively and in the present, accept all peoples of the world as members of one human family, that we seek world peace through world law, that we abandon prejudices of all kinds, and that we act always for the benefit of the whole human race. Quite a challenge!

• ***The Unity of all Religions:*** Baha'is believe that all religions come from God. That is simple but, for many, very hard to understand.

There is not only "one true religion." All religions teach deep spiritual truths. Baha'is accept the divine origins of: Hinduism, Buddhism, Judaism, Christianity, Islam, and all other faiths. The sacred scriptures of these faith traditions are holy. The spiritual practices of all religions—their traditions of prayer, meditation, service, and sacrifice—will all lead to growth and enlightenment. Baha'is believe that all of the great world religions were sent by God, at different times, and to different places with teachings tailored to the needs of the people. All of these religions have brought spiritual teachings for the guidance of the individual and social teachings to carry forward an advancing civilization.

The spiritual teachings of all religions are the same. All teach us to love, to be kind and generous, to pray and to reflect on our lives. All religions share the teachings of mercy, compassion, generosity, trustworthiness, honesty, truthfulness, modesty, charity, and so forth.

And, naturally, all religions differ according to the needs of the society in which they appeared. But these differences are all in the non-essential areas of language, ritual, clothing, restrictions on food, social customs, etc. These outward differences should not blind us to the deeper spiritual unity to be found among all religions. All of the Prophets of God—Buddha, Moses, Jesus, Muhammad—appeared in the world for the education of humanity: to develop immature souls to maturity, to teach spiritual truths, to exalt moral principles, and to quicken the conscience of humankind. They should all be equally revered.

These three ideas are basic. But there is more.

• **A World Community:** Baha'is believe in community. There are now Baha'is living in every country on earth. Baha'is have come together as an organized, world community to work for the principles of peace and unity. Baha'is try to practice the laws and teachings of their religion and offer these teachings to others for the betterment of the world.

• *Baha'u'llah, a Modern Prophet:* The Baha'i Faith is not just a collection of philosophical principles. The Baha'i community is not just a group of well-meaning people. Baha'is are followers of Baha'u'llah. Baha'is believe that, only a few years ago, a new prophet was sent into the world by God to guide humanity in this modern age. Baha'u'llah [pronounced: bah-HA o-LAH] stands at the center of Baha'i belief. Baha'is believe that this new divine teacher has brought us the spiritual tools by which we can construct a new world based on the principles of unity—the unity of God, the unity of religion, and the unity of humanity.

This book begins with the story of Baha'u'llah.

THE EDITORS

PART One

The Story of Baha'u'llah

*The aim of this Wronged One
in sustaining woes and tribulations . . .
hath been naught but to quench
the flame of hate and enmity,
that the horizon of the hearts of men
may be illumined with the light of concord
and attain real peace and tranquility.*

—Baha'u'llah[1]

STREET OF TEHRAN NEAR THE SIYYAH-CHAL, C. 1852

CHAPTER 1

First Light:
The Dawn of a New Age

> *I was but a man like others . . . when lo, the breezes of the All-Glorious were wafted over Me, and taught Me the knowledge of all that hath been. This thing is not from Me, but from One Who is Almighty and All-Knowing.*
>
> —Baha'u'llah[2]

HE MARCHED FOR MILES in chains toward the gates of the city. The August heat shimmered the horizon and scorched the stones under his bare and bleeding feet. The rhythmic clink of the prisoner's chains, the hoof-beats of the guards' horses, faded against the rowdy curses of a growing mob. The rabble gathered, happy to see a nobleman taste humiliation. Stones pelted him as he made his way past the city gates through the dirty streets of Tehran.

An old woman could not keep pace with the guards. She begged them to slow down long enough for her to throw the stone she had clutched in her fist. She cried out in frustration as the guards shoved past her. Then, the prisoner himself stopped and pleaded her cause. "Suffer not this woman to be disappointed," he told them. "Deny her not what she regards as a meritorious act in the sight of God."[3]

The guards had often witnessed fear, shock, anger and even violence in the people they had arrested over the years. And yet this prisoner's calm dignity remained, even in the face of rough treatment and abuses of the mob. He came from a wealthy and noble family of Tehran. His name was Mirza Husayn-'Ali, known later as Baha'u'llah (Arabic: the Glory of God). In another part of the same city, his wife and children did not know that he had been arrested or that he was being taken to the most notorious prison in Persia, the Siyah-Chal—the Black Pit.

The guards opened the door to the pit and the prisoner descended to the underbelly of Tehran. There was no light and no ventilation in this dungeon that had once been used as an underground reservoir. This prison in reality was nothing more than a narrow, stone hole in the ground extending twenty meters into the darkness. Within this dungeon, nearly one hundred fifty men lay in chains. They were starving, filthy, and deprived of all human dignity. The unbearable stench of the place oppressed these men whose lives seemed to have come to such a pathetic end. They were burdened as much by the hopelessness of their situation as by the skittering vermin that tormented them day and night.

The prisoners were seated in two rows facing each other on the bare stone floor, their feet linked by chains. Baha'u'llah was placed among them and fastened into shackles that were bolted to the floor. Across his neck was placed a chain that weighed about one hundred pounds. For the first three days of his imprisonment, he was given no food or drink. Sleep was impossible under the weight of the chains and surrounded by the incessant cries of pain and despair from the prisoners.

Why were these men treated so cruelly? Some were imprisoned for their crimes. There were thieves and murderers there. Others, such as Baha'u'llah, were imprisoned for their beliefs. These prisoners of conscience were the Babis, members of a new spiritual movement.

The Babi religion enraged the Muslim clergy because it proclaimed that religion must be renewed from time to time in a Divine Springtime. The physical seasons must change: Our lives depend on it. The Babis taught that our spiritual lives also depend on change and growth. Eventually, winter must end as new life awakens and pushes through the stagnant earth. The Babis believed that the time had come for a spiritual awakening, that new spiritual ideas must push aside outdated

> In the soil of whose heart will these holy seeds germinate? From the garden of whose soul will the blossoms of the invisible realities spring forth?
> —Baha'u'llah[4]

First Light: Dawn of a New Age

dogma. In a society steeped in the belief that Muhammad was the last of all prophets, and that Islam was the final and greatest of all religions, this was blasphemy. In Persia in the mid-1800s, there was no such thing as religious freedom. Despite this, Baha'u'llah and his companions fearlessly proclaimed their Faith to anyone who would listen.

NAVVAB, THE WIFE OF BAHA'U'LLAH, learned of her husband's arrest when a servant suddenly rushed into her presence in great distress. "He is arrested!—I have seen him!" the servant cried. "He has walked many miles! O they have beaten him! . . . His feet are bleeding! . . . There are chains upon his neck."[5] Soon, everyone knew of Baha'u'llah's arrest and the family home was ransacked by mobs. Navvab gathered what she could and escaped with her children into hiding. She knew very well that Babi women and children had been murdered by mobs many times before.

Once she and her husband had worked side by side to help the poor. Now, she had become one of the homeless. To purchase food for the children, she sold some gold buttons from her clothing. At times she had nothing to offer her children to eat but a bit of dry flour that she poured into the palms of their hands. Despite their own dangerous situation, the family's greatest anxiety was about Baha'u'llah: Was he alive? Was he being tortured?

After a few days the family learned where he was being held. Baha'u'llah's oldest son Abbas, later known as 'Abdu'l-Baha, then eight years old, could not be held back. He persuaded a servant who worked for the family to take him to see his father. The servant took the boy to the prison and carried him on his shoulders down the stairs into the pit. As they descended into the darkness, they could see nothing. Suddenly, they heard the voice of Baha'u'llah command, "Do not bring him!"

Immediately, they turned around and walked back out. 'Abdu'l-Baha then learned from the guards that the prisoners were to be taken outside briefly for their meal. He waited until noon when, filthy and ragged (some were even naked), the men were filed out of the pit. Then he saw his father: bent over from the chains, his neck bruised and swollen from a heavy steel collar, clothes tattered, hair and beard disheveled, his face pale and gaunt. At some point during his imprisonment, Baha'u'llah had been poisoned and his appearance dramatically showed its effects. The child fainted from the shock. He had to be carried away.

THE AUTHORITIES HOPED that placing Baha'u'llah in the black pit would put an end to his life, his faith, or both. But the dungeon did not crush him, it helped create him. Those who knew Baha'u'llah had always expected some future greatness from him. Baha'u'llah's father had been a minister at the court of the shah. When his father died, he was offered a position at the court. When he heard that Baha'u'llah had declined the offer, the Prime Minister remarked: "Leave him to himself. Such a position is unworthy of him. He has some higher aim in view. I cannot understand him, but I am convinced that he is destined for some lofty career. His thoughts are not like ours. Let him alone."[6]

Now, in the darkness of the pit, there dawned within Baha'u'llah a revolutionary vision so intense that its light would spread from this dungeon in Tehran over the course of time to virtually every location on earth. Baha'u'llah described his spiritual state while in the black pit:

> During the days I lay in the prison of Tehran, though the galling weight of the chains and the stench-filled air allowed Me but little sleep, still in those infrequent moments of slumber I felt as if something flowed from the crown of My head over My breast, even as a mighty torrent that precipitateth itself upon the earth from the summit of a lofty mountain. Every limb of My body would, as a result, be set afire. At such moments My tongue recited what no man could bear to hear.[7]

Further describing this vision, Baha'u'llah used the symbol of a Maiden sent from heaven—a sign of wisdom, spiritual insight, and universal truth:

While engulfed in tribulations I heard a most wondrous, a

most sweet voice, calling above My head. Turning My face, I beheld a Maiden—the embodiment of the remembrance of the name of My Lord—suspended in the air before Me. . . . She was imparting to both My inward and outer being tidings which rejoiced My soul, and the souls of God's honored servants. Pointing with her finger unto My head, she addressed all who are in heaven and all who are on earth, saying: "By God! This is the Best-Beloved of the worlds, and yet ye comprehend not. This is the Beauty of God amongst you, and the power of His sovereignty within you, could ye but understand. This is the Mystery of God and His Treasure, the Cause of God and His glory unto all who are in the kingdoms of Revelation and of creation, if ye be of them that perceive."[8]

Throughout history, great souls have felt an unrelenting desire to spiritually uplift their people. There came in each one's life a moment, such as this one, when that calling was heard and could not be denied.

Moses experienced such a moment. Fear and trembling engulfed him when he found the Burning Bush and spoke to the voice of God. When Jesus rose from his baptism in the river Jordan, the Gospel tells us that the heavens opened. A heavenly dove—another symbol of the spirit—spoke to him and announced his destiny. Muhammad saw an angel

> O my children!
> I fear lest, bereft of the melody of the dove of heaven, ye will sink back to the shades of utter loss, and, never having gazed upon the beauty of the rose, return to water and clay.
> —Baha'u'llah[9]

First Light: Dawn of a New Age

while he was praying in the mountains near his home. He ran and hid in his wife's lap after the terror of seeing the vision of Gabriel, who commanded him to recite the verses given to him by God. We can never understand the full meaning of these events, nor of Baha'u'llah's vision of the Maiden. And yet, it is our nature to wonder.

Before the Budddha's enlightenment under the tree of bodhi, he was lost in questions: Why is there so much suffering? What is the point of living, knowing that it will result in old age, pain, and death? Philosophies and religions alike have wrestled with these unanswerable questions: Who are we? Why are we here? In the words of the author of Ecclesiastes, "As you do not know how the spirit comes to the bones in the womb of a woman with child, so you do not know the work of God who makes everything."[10]

A man is born in an ordinary place and time, with brothers and sisters and all appearances of an ordinary life. As he grows to manhood, something within him awakens and calls him with such intensity that he casts aside the comfort and safety of his family and his home to pursue another path. Baha'u'llah gave us his own description of this phenomenon in a letter addressed to the Shah of Persia:

> O King! I was but a man like others. . . . when lo, the breezes of the All-Glorious were wafted over Me, and taught Me the knowledge of all that hath been. This thing

is not from Me, but from One Who is Almighty and All-Knowing. And He bade Me lift up My voice between earth and heaven, and for this there befell Me what hath caused the tears of every man of understanding to flow.

The learning current amongst men I studied not; their schools I entered not. Ask of the city wherein I dwelt, that thou mayest be well assured that I am not of them who speak falsely. This is but a leaf which the winds of the will of thy Lord, the Almighty, the All-Praised, have stirred. Can it be still when the tempestuous winds are blowing? Nay, by Him Who is the Lord of all Names and Attributes! They move it as they list.

The evanescent is as nothing before Him Who is the Ever-Abiding. His all-compelling summons hath reached Me, and caused Me to speak His praise amidst all people. I was indeed as one dead when His behest was uttered. The hand of the will of thy Lord, the Compassionate, the Merciful, transformed Me.[11]

The men imprisoned with Baha'u'llah were the first to catch the spark of his newly ignited faith. Baha'u'llah taught the men to chant two verses, in a call-and-response manner as they sat facing each other in the darkness:

"God is sufficient unto me; He verily is the All-Sufficing!" chanted one row.

The other responded, "In Him let the trusting trust . . ."

When Baha'u'llah had first

> God is sufficient unto me; He verily is the All-Sufficing! In Him let the trusting trust.
> —Baha'u'llah[12]

First Light: Dawn of a New Age

entered the black pit, nothing could be heard but cries of despair and pain, the rattling of chains, and the scurrying of rats. Now the chanting of the men praising God could be heard well beyond the prison grounds.

Even the king in his nearby palace heard the singing. One day in an absurdly hypocritical gesture, the shah sent a tray of roast lamb to Baha'u'llah and the men in the dungeon. We can only imagine how enticing the sight and smell of the food was to the starving men. All of them turned to Baha'u'llah to see what his reaction would be. Baha'u'llah returned the tray to the shah untouched, and the men resumed their singing. They had achieved such a state of detachment that only one of them expressed any regret at turning down the lamb.

The guards went beyond physical torture, to apply cruel psychological tactics in their attempts to break the resolve of the Babis. On one occasion the guards selected a Babi for execution, took him away and then brought him back, stating that this one was too skinny to execute. They exchanged him for another man and led him to his death.

No matter what happened, the new spirit of the prison could not be broken. Each day, the guards entered the black pit and called out the name of one Babi. That one would first embrace Baha'u'llah, and then follow the guards to the place of his execution.

To the followers of Baha'u'llah, life is sacred because all of creation reflects the beauty of the Creator. And yet when death comes, it is viewed as a doorway to reunion with God. As Baha'u'llah taught, "I have made death a messenger of joy to thee. Wherefore dost thou grieve? I made the light to shed on thee its splendor. Why dost thou veil thyself therefrom?"[13]

BAHA'U'LLAH'S WIFE AND CHILDREN understood the danger he faced while in prison. Each morning brought with it the death of one more Babi. With each passing day, they wondered if Baha'u'llah would survive to the next.

'ABDU'L-BAHA AS A YOUNG MAN

CHAPTER 2

Banished:
Exile to Baghdad

Were their oppressors to be asked: "Wherefore have ye oppressed them and held them in bondage in Baghdad and elsewhere?" . . . they would know not what to answer. Thou knowest full well, O my God, that their only crime is to have loved Thee.
—Baha'u'llah[1]

FOR FOUR MONTHS, family and friends of Baha'u'llah time and again pleaded for his freedom. Each time their pleas were denied. Russian Prince Dimitri Dolgorukov, who was serving as an ambassador to Tehran, knew Baha'u'llah personally. The prince's secretary was Baha'u'llah's brother-in-law. They appealed Baha'u'llah's imprisonment at the court. He declared that he was extending the protection of the Russian government to Baha'u'llah. Soon the shah reluctantly issued an order to release Baha'u'llah from prison.

Before his release from the black pit, Baha'u'llah was interrogated one more time. An envoy was sent to retrieve Baha'u'llah. Tears came to his eyes when he saw the horrible conditions in which this noble and innocent man had been imprisoned. He took off his own cloak to place it over the tattered clothing of Baha'u'llah for his appearance at the court. However, Baha'u'llah refused the covering offered him and presented himself at the court as he was.

The Grand Vizier addressed Baha'u'llah with the admonition that if he had stopped associating himself with the Faith of the Bab, as the vizier had advised him previously, Baha'u'llah would not have had so much suffering. If the powers of state had hoped that the black pit would break his spirit and diminish his resolve, they soon found out that the opposite had occurred. Baha'u'llah answered that had the vizier followed his advice, "the affairs of the government would not have reached so critical a stage!"

At this point the vizier recalled a conversation that took place after the execution of the founder of the Babi movement in which Baha'u'llah had told him, "The flame that has been kindled will blaze forth more fiercely than ever." Realizing that this is exactly what had happened, the vizier asked Baha'u'llah what he should do next. Baha'u'llah requested that he: "Command the governors of this realm to cease shedding the blood of the innocent, to cease plundering their property, to cease dishonoring their women and injuring their children. Let them cease the persecution of the Faith of the Bab."[2] The Vizier did stop the oppression of the Babis for a time. It was only a short interruption, though, in a series of persecutions that would last for over 150 years.

THE BABI RELIGION began nine years earlier in 1844, in Shiraz. A prophetic figure named 'Ali-Muhammad claimed to be the gate through which a new cycle of human enlightenment would arrive. He took the title "The Bab" (Arabic: Gate) and so his followers were known as Babis. Much like John the Baptist in an earlier time, the Bab preached a message of individual spirituality and an unfolding of social progress. Also like the earlier prophet, he was eventually killed for his beliefs.

The Bab initially attracted eighteen followers, one of whom was a woman, called Tahirih, who was the daughter of a prominent Islamic scholar. Her father educated her at home and often remarked that if she had only been born a boy she would have brought great honor to his house. When she encountered the teachings of this new Faith, she eagerly embraced them. Her father bitterly opposed them.

Also known as Quratu'l-'Ayn, Tahirih was a spiritual

> For a long time now, I have thirsted after this; I have yearned for these explanations, these inner truths. Give me whatever you have of these books. Never mind if it angers my father.
> —Tahirih[3]

Banished: Exile to Baghdad 17

and poetic genius who became an outspoken advocate of
the new Faith, despite living in a time and place when
women were to be neither seen nor heard. During one
Babi conference, she wished to demonstrate the casting
off of the old traditions and entrance into a new era of
enlightenment. She did this by taking off her outer covering (her veil) during the conference and revealing her
face. This caused a violent reaction from some of the
men who were unprepared to accept the emancipation of
women as part of the social progress they had been advo-
cating. Baha'u'llah defended her actions and was in fact
the one who gave her the title Tahirih (Arabic: the Pure
One). Tahirih was eventually executed by the Persian
government, as were most of the Babi leaders. Before she
was killed, she is reported to have said, "You can kill me
as soon as you like, but you cannot stop the emancipation of women." 4

THE BABI FAITH attracted people from every sector of
society: wealthy merchants as well as tradesmen, religious
scholars and illiterates, people who hungered for an
inner spiritual awakening, and those who thirsted for
social revolution in those oppressive times.

Baha'u'llah became a proponent of this movement at
the age of twenty-seven when a Babi sent him some of
the writings of the Bab. Although he sought no leadership role in the community, Baha'u'llah was soon widely

recognized as one of its most distinguished supporters, a recognition that placed his life in danger. Muhammad Shah issued a death warrant against Baha'u'llah, even though his only crime was following a religion opposed by the state. The warrant expired, however, upon the sudden death of the king himself in 1848.

Becoming a Babi meant putting everything at risk: your life, your family, your property, the good graces of friends and relatives. Some clergymen preached from their pulpits that to murder a Babi and steal his property were acts of righteousness. Many from the largely uneducated masses sought their moment of glory in what became the blood sport of Babi killing. Baha'u'llah wrote, "Religious fanaticism and hatred are a world-devouring fire, whose violence none can quench."[5] Thousands of Babi men, women, and children were killed. The government officials offered no protection to the Babis. In fact, they were as outraged as the Muslim clergy at the disruption to society that this religious upheaval had caused.

Persia at this time was ruled by a shared power system of the shah and the Islamic clergy. These two forces had virtually unchecked power over human life. The public executions they ordered were perversely inventive. Westerners in Persia were so revolted by the massacres of the Babis that occured on the streets that some resigned their positions and left the country. Others remained in their homes to avoid witnessing horrors such as men being beheaded, flayed, drawn and quartered, having molten lead poured down their throats or lit candles placed into carved-out holes of their flesh, or being shod like horses and forced to run through the streets.

The Babi movement swept through Persia like a wildfire, converting nobles and commoners alike. On the other side were the powers of the state and the mobs of fundamentalist fanatics who violently stamped out this fire anywhere they found it. As soon as a significant number of people in a village became Babis, they would be destroyed. As soon as a prominent person joined this cause, he would be mowed down. As Baha'u'llah lay in the Siyah-Chal, many of the other Babi leaders were killed or traveled from village to village teaching this new Faith while staying one step ahead of death. The Babi Faith faced powerful opposition and was forced underground. In prison, Baha'u'llah felt called to revive and direct this persecuted movement:

> One night, in a dream, these exalted words were heard on every side: "Verily, We shall render Thee victorious by Thyself and by Thy Pen. Grieve Thou not for that which hath befallen Thee, neither be Thou afraid, for Thou art in safety. Ere long will God raise up the treasures of the earth—men who will aid Thee . . ." 6

AT LAST BAHA'U'LLAH WAS RELEASED and allowed to return to his family. Soon after that came an order from the shah that he leave Persia within one month. The order of exile banished him for life. His land and all other possessions were confiscated by the government. What the mobs had not stolen by riot, the Prime Minister now took by fiat. He transferred the deeds to some of Baha'u'llah's properties to his own name.

As the family considered the difficulties of travel to Baghdad in winter, they feared that Navvab's youngest child, Mihdi, would not survive the exile. He was very young and in delicate health. For his protection, his parents reluctantly left him in the care of relatives in Persia. It would be several years before he was able to rejoin his parents.

The exile of Baha'u'llah from Persia to Iraq was a three-month, six hundred-mile journey, from January to April. The men and older children in the party of exiles walked, or rode on horseback. Navvab and her young daughter Bahiyyih, as well as other women among the exiles, rode in howdahs. A howdah was a wooden seat perched on a mule and covered with an enclosed canopy.

The winter was severe, particularly as they passed over the mountains. The exiles had not been able to buy adequate clothing before they left. 'Abdu'l-Baha's hands and feet were frost-bitten from riding all day in the cold. The raw stark beauty of winter in the mountains, the difficult conditions, the uncertainty of what lay ahead, the joy of having Baha'u'llah with them again, all mingled together in this journey.

As spring approached, they had the mountain passes

behind them and easier travel ahead. They were able to camp in an orange grove in full blossom for the Persian new year holiday in March. Despite being an exile banished by his government and escorted by mounted guards from Persia, Baha'u'llah continued to teach the Faith through villages as they traveled. As they passed from Persia to Iraq, Baha'u'llah found followers among the Kurds and Arabs. Some of the Arab and Kurdish followers traveled with them to the gates of Baghdad.

Baghdad in 1853 was a major city of the Ottoman empire, well-known for its great mosques and city squares. Baha'u'llah settled into a house in the old quarter of Baghdad.

THE FLAME KINDLED by the Bab and fueled by the hopes and lives of so many Babis was now nearly extinguished. The believers were few and scattered; many who had not lost their lives had lost their hope. The Babi leaders were mostly killed. Perhaps they had all died in vain. After nearly a year in Baghdad, without telling anyone of his intention, Baha'u'llah left one morning for the mountains of Kurdistan near Sulaymaniyyih. In his words, it was a separation that "hoped for no return."

CHAPTER 3

Solitude:
In Kurdistan

> *Those who are near unto Thee have been abandoned in the darkness of desolation: Where is the shining of the morn of Thy reunion, O Desire of the worlds?*
>
> —Baha'u'llah[1]

AFTER LEAVING BAGHDAD, Baha'u'llah lived alone in the wilderness, at times in a cave or in a crude rock shelter. Despite the physical deprivation, despite his grief over the decline of the Babi community, his soul spent blissful days in communion with God. In that loneliness his soul was free to be filled with the completeness of the love of God. The solitude that Baha'u'llah sought in the inhospitable mountains of Kurdistan reminds us of Moses wandering on Mount

Sinai, or the communion Jesus sought with his Heavenly Father on the Mount of Olives. God spoke to Moses when he was alone on the mountain. Muhammad returned time and again to the mountains seeking the refuge of prayer.

MONTHS INTO HIS RETREAT, Baha'u'llah one day encountered a young boy sitting by the side of the road, crying. He stopped to ask the boy what had made him cry. The child's teacher had instructed each student to copy a certain passage. The child had lost the paper he was supposed to copy and now feared his teacher's punishment. Baha'u'llah sat down and wrote a few verses for the boy, and he happily ran to school. The child's teacher was astonished at the calligraphy the boy showed him and surprised that this work of art came from the solitary hermit they knew as Darvish Muhammad. The fragment of Baha'u'llah's writing made its way to the head of the local Sufi community. Intrigued by the calligraphy, the Sufi Shaykh began a friendship with Baha'u'llah. Soon he became a loved and respected figure among the Sufis of Kurdistan.

Stories of Darvish Muhammad spread from Sulaymaniyyih to Baghdad. In time, the family of Baha'u'llah realized that Darvish Muhammad must be Baha'u'llah. They sent a messenger to find him and beg him to return. His two years of seclusion came to an end in March of 1856, when he returned to Baghdad. He did not wish to return, but submitted his will to the calling he felt from God to revive the community that had lost both its integrity and its direction. In describing the futility of escaping the course that had been destined for him, Baha'u'llah acknowledged:

> . . . the mesh of divine destiny exceedeth the vastest of mortal conceptions, and the dart of His decree transcendeth the boldest of human designs. None can escape the snares He setteth, and no soul can find release except through submission to His will.[2]

Moses was commanded by God to leave Mount Sinai and go back to his people when they returned to their pagan roots to worship a golden calf. Jesus retreated to the Mount of Olives to grieve over the death of John the Baptist. He was impelled to come down from the mountain, though, by the pressing needs of the people for his teaching and his healing.

Baha'u'llah's daughter Bahiyyih recalled the family's loneliness during his absence. Her brother 'Abdu'l-Baha, during this time, would often go off by himself, and the family would find him weeping. At other times, he kept himself busy transcribing the writings of the Bab. When Baha'u'llah returned they hardly recognized him, so much had his physical appearance changed during two years in the wilderness. In a heart-rending reunion, 'Abdu'l-Baha fell at Baha'u'llah's feet as father and son wept together.

Solitude: In Kurdistan

When Baha'u'llah encountered the Babis, he "found no more than a handful of souls, faint and dispirited, nay utterly lost and dead. The Cause of God had ceased to be on any one's lips, nor was any heart receptive to its message."[3]

Many Sufis came from Kurdistan to visit Baha'u'llah. Although prejudice of class, nationality and religion ran strong in that society, at his home in Baghdad he had guests every day from all ranks and classes of Jewish, Christian, and Muslim backgrounds. Many adversaries were won over as much by his kindness as by the clarity of his arguments. One prince of Persia who visited with Baha'u'llah said, "I know not how to explain it, were all the sorrows of the world to be crowded into my heart they would, I feel, all vanish, when in the presence of Baha'u'llah. It is as if I had entered Paradise itself." [4]

BAHA'U'LLAH WAS WELL AWARE during this time of the intention of certain government officials and religious clergy to harm him. Despite this, he remained serene and wrote some of his most important works. One of these is the Hidden Words, a short book composed of aphorisms written as the voice of God Himself speaking to the human heart and mind. Composed mainly while Baha'u'llah was walking along the banks of the Tigris, this work speaks to us that we were created out of the love of God, and this love is our true life:

O Son of Man!
I loved thy creation, hence I created thee. Wherefore, do thou love Me, that I may name thy name and fill thy soul with the spirit of life.

O Son of Spirit!
Noble have I created thee, yet thou hast abased thyself. Rise then unto that for which thou wast created.

O Son of Man!
Rejoice in the gladness of thine heart, that thou mayest be worthy to meet Me and to mirror forth My beauty.

O Son of Being!
Busy not thyself with this world, for with fire We test the gold, and with gold We test Our servants.[5]

THE GROWING INFLUENCE OF BAHA'U'LLAH could clearly be seen in the number of people who came to hear him speak. It was even more evident in the spiritual renewal he brought about in the Babis. He taught them to avoid divisive politics, to obey just governments, be trustworthy and honest, to love their fellow man and be charitable, and to surrender their wills to the Will of God.

The writings of Baha'u'llah also had a great effect on the spirituality of the Babis. Another of his major works written while in Baghdad is the Kitab-i Iqan, or the Book of Certitude, which upholds the unity of God and His

Messengers. This book portrays the great religions as being revealed by the same God; they are part of one process of spiritual education. The book in particular highlights the connections between Judaism, Christianity, and Islam. Dictated over the course of two days, this remarkable work models a unique foundation on which unity between the religions can be built.

Judaism, Christianity, and Islam trace their heritage back to Abraham. Arabs and Jews are descendants of Abraham through his sons Ishmael and Isaac, respectively. Moses, Jesus and Muhammad all claim Abraham as their forefather. Baha'u'llah created a new vision of these founders of the Abrahamic religions, whose followers see them as competing prophets. Wars have been fought for centuries in attempts to prove the superiority of one faith over another. Baha'u'llah did not see them as competitors. He saw them as Divine Educators in the same school of religion. They were sent by the same God to different peoples at different times to help them progress both spiritually and materially. They speak in two ways. In one type of speech, they give spiritual and ethical teachings that are universal and timeless. In another type of speech, they give teachings for a specific time and people to help them advance.

> The purpose of these Educators, in all they said and taught, was to preserve man's exalted station.
> —Baha'u'llah[6]

The prophets of God give the same ethical teachings in every age. Their specific prescriptions for living vary from age to age, however, because the needs of each time are different. In the words of Baha'u'llah, these prophets of God are:

> . . . all sent down from the heaven of the Will of God, and as they all arise to proclaim His irresistible Faith, they therefore are regarded as one soul and the same person. For they all drink from the one Cup of the love of God, and all partake of the fruit of the same Tree of Oneness.[7]

IN BAGHDAD, BAHA'U'LLAH'S LIFE was threatened on several occasions but he seemed remarkably undisturbed by these attempts. On one occasion, a member of the Persian consulate hired an assassin to murder Baha'u'llah. The assassin, named Reza Turk, approached Baha'u'llah as he walked along the banks of the Tigris. When he came face to face with Baha'u'llah, he fumbled and dropped his gun. Baha'u'llah turned to one of his companions and told him to pick up the man's gun, hand it back to him, and point him towards his home, remarking, "He seems to have lost his way."

Baha'u'llah took a daily walk to one of the local coffee houses in Baghdad where men typically gathered. Whichever coffee house he went to prospered as local clerics, government officials, merchants, and others crowded around him.

As admiration for Baha'u'llah increased from the

townspeople as well as from people coming in from Persia, the Persian consul-general in Baghdad and the Shi'ite clergy became increasingly agitated since they thought the Babi movement had been crushed. Also, the clergy were distressed that Baha'u'llah lived so near the Shi'ite holy places that are located near Baghdad. They tried to persuade the Ottoman Sultan to extradite him back to Persia where they could do with him as they pleased. The Sultan had heard numerous reports over the years of the noble character of Baha'u'llah, and he refused to extradite him. He did, however, forward a message that Baha'u'llah would, as a guest of the Ottoman government, be asked to move farther from Persia to Constantinople (modern-day Istanbul).

This message was forwarded to the governor of Baghdad who was an admirer of Baha'u'llah. The governor ignored the order for three months because he felt ashamed to give such a message to a man he admired so deeply. Finally, after receiving five successive orders of banishment, he sent his deputy to meet with Baha'u'llah and give him the news that he was to be exiled to Constantinople. Baha'u'llah accepted the order of banishment without protest. He took the sum of money the government gave him to pay for his transport and distributed it to the poor.

CHAPTER 4

Paradise:
The Garden of Ridvan

> *In the darksome night of despair, my eye turneth expectant and full of hope to the morn of Thy boundless favor and at the hour of dawn, my drooping soul is refreshed and strengthened in remembrance of Thy beauty and perfection.*
> —'Abdu'l-Baha[1]

The news of Baha'u'llah's banishment swept through Baghdad like a sandstorm. The Babi community was greatly distressed at the thought of Baha'u'llah leaving them. In every way, he was the heart of their community. The house of Baha'u'llah was too small for all the visitors who crowded in to see him one more time. Plus, the constant stream of visitors put an added burden on Navvab who was trying to pack and prepare for the journey. A prominent man of Baghdad offered his private garden outside of town as a place where

Baha'u'llah could meet with visitors. This park was later called the Garden of Ridvan (Paradise; pronounced Rez-vahn) by Baha'u'llah's followers.

On April 22, 1863, Baha'u'llah left his house in Baghdad for the last time, walking toward the river that he would cross on his way to the garden. It was an emotional and memorable scene. People packed the streets and some climbed up on the rooftops to get one last look at Baha'u'llah. In the center of this whirlwind was the calm figure of Baha'u'llah.

His followers gathered in the Garden of Ridvan, outside the gates of Baghdad, for twelve days. Although Baha'u'llah had not shared with anyone the nature of his transforming experience in the black pit of Tehran ten years earlier, many had recognized his station on their own. They recognized this in the spontaneous outpouring of his speech that seemed to come from an innate and superior wisdom, his calm dignity in the face of either praise from notables or assassination attempts by enemies. Moreover it was something they felt in his presence, a radiant love that inspired them towards the highest standards of morality and kindness. Now to his followers, Baha'u'llah announced the nature of his mission, an announcement that caused great joy to those who had already sensed it, and a renewed sense of purpose to all of them.

Every morning in the Ridvan Garden, the gardeners picked roses and piled them in the center of Baha'u'llah's tent. In gestures of friendship, Baha'u'llah would give a rose to each visitor, and others to be taken to his Arab and Persian friends in Baghdad.

Nightingales sang during the evenings as they nested among the rose bushes. Baha'u'llah compared their beautiful songs and their love of the roses to the passionate devotion of a life lived in service to God. For love of the roses, he observed, the nightingales sing their most beautiful songs in the darkest hour. In the same way, those who love God and his creation will offer their gifts to humanity, despite the darkness that surrounds them.

Those who visited Baha'u'llah in the Garden of Ridvan noticed that he never complained of his treatment by the government. His only thought seemed to be of weaving ties of fellowship among the citizens of Baghdad.

BAHA'U'LLAH LEFT BAGHDAD in a caravan of fifty mules, several horses and ten armed Ottoman guards. He shared the one-hundred-ten-day journey with his family and twenty-six of his followers who were allowed to go into exile with him. The Governor of Baghdad ordered that they should be hosted at each village in which they stopped on the way. Baha'u'llah arrived in Constantinople, the capital of the Turkish Empire in August of 1863.

It was the custom then for people visiting the capital to call on ministers and try to obtain an audience with the sultan. For most Persians there, this was a means of social climbing, political maneuvering, or of begging favors from ministers. In contrast, Baha'u'llah chose not to call on any ministers or officials. He did not return the visits of those that called on him. The Persian ambassador used Baha'u'llah's refusal to bow his knee before his oppressor as a means of swaying opinion against him at the court. The ambassador's interpretation of Baha'u'llah's actions was to present him as a lawless agitator who felt himself above authority and who should be regarded as a danger to both the Persian and Turkish thrones. The ambassador's four-month rumor campaign succeeded: the sultan issued another edict of banishment against Baha'u'llah.

Almost immediately Baha'u'llah, his family, and a dozen companions were sent to Adrianople (now Edirne, in European Turkey). Armed officers placed them and their belongings in crude carts and marched them through twelve days of frozen, barren terrain. That winter was unusually severe, and the exiles did not have adequate clothing to protect them from the elements. They had to build fires to melt ice from the frozen rivers to get drinking water. On the road, they saw several people frozen to death. When they arrived in Adrianople, they stayed in a caravanserai, then were moved to a small home. Baha'u'llah's daughter described the conditions of the house:

That winter was a period of intense suffering, due to cold, hunger, and, above all, to the torments of vermin, with which the house was swarming. These made even the days horrible, and the nights still more so. When they were so intolerable that it was impossible to sleep, my brother ['Abdu'l-Baha] would light a lamp (which somewhat intimidated the vermin) and by singing and laughing seek to restore the spirits of the family.[2]

ADRIANOPLE WAS THE FARTHEST FROM PERSIA that Baha'u'llah was exiled. After a few months in Adrianople, Baha'u'llah moved to a house near the great mosque of Sultan Salim. Once again the exiles settled into a new location, keeping themselves busy and earning their livelihood with the various trades and businesses that Baha'u'llah had encouraged them to pursue.

Baha'u'llah spent five years in Adrianople. In Constantinople and then in Adrianople, Baha'u'llah met less with public officials than he had in Baghdad. Instead, Baha'u'llah's eldest son 'Abdu'l-Baha, now a young man, took those tasks upon himself. The writings of Baha'u'llah increased in volume and broadened in scope. It was in Adrianople that Baha'u'llah began to write to the kings and rulers of the world.

In these tablets, Baha'u'llah challenged the rulers of his time to use their power to help their people, rather than for conquest. Baha'u'llah wrote that the purpose of their power was to bring about justice. If they could not use their power for justice, then it was empty and useless:

> God hath committed into your hands the reins of the government of the people, that ye may rule with justice over them, safeguard the rights of the downtrodden, and punish wrong-doers.[3]

> If ye stay not the hand of the oppressor, if ye fail to safeguard the rights of the downtrodden, what right have ye then to vaunt yourselves among men?[4]

He also questioned the justice of taxing people to pay for palaces:

> O Kings of the earth! We see you increasing every year your expenditures, and laying the burden thereof on your subjects. This, verily, is wholly and grossly unjust. Fear the sighs and tears of this Wronged One, and lay not excessive burdens on your peoples. Do not rob them to rear palaces for yourselves; nay rather choose for them that which ye choose for yourselves.[5]

Baha'u'llah pointed out the negative effects of excessive military spending. Rulers should try to settle their differences peacefully, rather than increase the military:

> Compose your differences, and reduce your armaments, that the burden of your expenditures may be lightened, and that your minds and hearts may be tranquillized. Heal

the dissensions that divide you, and ye will no longer be in need of any armaments except what the protection of your cities and territories demandeth.[6]

All the monarchs ignored Baha'u'llah's messages. Queen Victoria is reported to have said, "If this is of God, it will endure; if not, it can do no harm."[7]

BAHA'U'LLAH HAD BEEN THE CENTER of the Babi community for many years. As time went on, his followers began calling themselves Baha'is (followers of Baha) rather than Babis (followers of the Bab). This was because they saw their Faith progressing to a new phase with the additional teachings given by Baha'u'llah. Most of the Babis of Persia became Baha'is through the influence of outstanding teachers who traveled throughout Persia sharing the writings and teachings of Baha'u'llah. These writings sustained the Baha'is to such a degree that these early believers were able to withstand great persecutions. Thousands were killed for their beliefs and faced their brutal and unjust executions with a steadfastness that astonished their oppressors.

The effect of Baha'u'llah on his followers was itself one of his greatest accomplishments. Not only did they bear the oppression they faced but also accomplished the much more difficult work of changing their hearts and minds.

Pardise: The Garden of Ridvan

A Baha'i named Haydar-'Ali related a story of his own spiritual education received from Baha'u'llah. One day this believer had purchased some tea that was to be used in the house of Baha'u'llah: In middle-eastern culture, the serving of tea is an important part of social life. People enjoy the fragrance and color of the steaming tea served in delicate glass cups. Apparently the tea that Haydar-'Ali purchased in Constantinople and sent to Adrianople was not of the finest quality. A member of the household in charge of provisions wrote to Haydar-'Ali and in a very kind manner encouraged him to purchase better quality tea in the future. Haydar-'Ali's pride was wounded by this unsolicited advice, and he wrote an insulting reply. Immediately after this, Haydar-'Ali received a letter from Baha'u'llah which was full of praise and encouragement. The letter assured him that Baha'u'llah had accepted all of his many services, expressing full approval and pleasure.

Upon reading this tablet, Haydar-'Ali was filled with remorse for his rude letter and his own arrogance that caused him to write it. Haydar-'Ali later wrote that he:

> . . . understood the way in which God works in this Most Great, this Most Ancient Revelation . . . and it is this: that in order to educate the sinners, edify the souls of the evil-doers, and teach them human virtues and the way of servitude, Baha'u'llah chastises them with the scourge of loving-kindness and compassion, of tender mercy and grace. To them He manifests His attributes of the All-Merciful, the Concealer of the faults of men. . . .[8]

MANY BAHA'IS FROM PERSIA came to Adrianople to see Baha'u'llah. This was noticed by the Persian authorities and caused them some concern. Also, the Persian authorities were offended that the governor and other high-ranking Ottoman officials showed such admiration for Baha'u'llah and 'Abdu'l-Baha.

In an Islamic cultural context, religion and politics are inevitably intertwined. Recall that the faith community of the Prophet Muhammad over the course of time became rulers over a great Islamic civilization. This is why this new religion was seen as a threat to the established political order even though Baha'u'llah clearly stated in his writings that he laid no claim to any territory other than the human heart.

> More grievous became Our plight from day to day, nay, from hour to hour, until they took Us forth from Our prison and made Us, with glaring injustice, enter the Most Great Prison.
> —Baha'u'llah[9]

Once more, the order of banishment came from the capital city of Istanbul. This time, Baha'u'llah was to be sent to an undisclosed location. Conditions there would be such that Baha'u'llah would later call it the "Most Great Prison."

THE PRISON CITY OF 'AKKA

CHAPTER 5

Final Exile:
The Most Desolate City

He Who hath come to build anew the whole world, behold, how they . . . have forced Him to dwell within the most desolate of cities!
—Baha'u'llah[1]

ONE MORNING the house of Baha'u'llah in Adrianople was surrounded by soldiers as the order for exile was carried out. Many of his followers were interrogated. Baha'u'llah described the situation as his followers were taken to prison and "were left on the first night without food. . . . The people surrounded the house, and Muslims and Christians wept over us. . . . We perceived that the weeping of the people of the Son (Christians) exceeded the weeping of others—a sign for such as ponder."[2]

One of the exiles recalled, "A great tumult seized the people. . . . Some expressed their sympathy, others consoled us, and wept over us. . . . Most of our possessions were auctioned at half their value."[3]

Several foreign ambassadors in Adrianople went to Baha'u'llah and offered to negotiate a reprieve with the sultan. Baha'u'llah expressed his appreciation for their kindness but refused their offers of political support.

On August 12, 1868, Baha'u'llah, his family, and the other exiles were taken by carriage to Gallipoli. At first, Baha'u'llah and his companions were not told where they were being sent or if they were to be separated and sent to different places. Later, the decision was announced that Baha'u'llah and seventy of his followers were to be sent to the remote penal colony of 'Akka in Palestine. Baha'u'llah warned his followers of the dangers that lay ahead, stating that "this journey will be unlike any of the previous journeys." He said that any of his followers who felt unprepared to face extreme hardship should "depart to whatever place he pleaseth, and be preserved from tests, for hereafter he will find himself unable to leave."[4] The companions of Baha'u'llah chose to go with him into exile, accepting whatever lay ahead, rather than be separated from Baha'u'llah.

From Gallipoli, the exiles took a steamer to Alexandria, Eygpt. Another steamer took them from Alexandria to Haifa (now in northern Israel). From there, a sailing vessel took them across the bay to 'Akka. The passage to 'Akka was quite exhausting due to the combined effects of the heat, sea sickness, the filthy conditions of the ships, and improper food.

The exiles arrived in 'Akka on August 31, 1868. There was no dock at the port of 'Akka. The Baha'i men were told to wade from the boat to the shore, and the women would be carried on the backs of the men. In the context of that Muslim culture, such an intimate physical contact between the women and the men would have been a great insult to the chastity and reputation of the women. 'Abdu'l-Baha insisted to the guards that the women be carried one at a time on a chair to the shore.

A rough crowd had gathered on the shore to jeer 'Akka's newest prisoners and their leader, whom they denounced as the "god of the Persians."

'Akka, called St. Jean d'Acre by the Crusaders centuries before, was now under the Ottoman Turks a flea-infested, desolate penal colony with a reputation for unhealthy air and water. The environment was so bad that a local proverb said that a bird flying over 'Akka would fall dead. Plagued by diseases that accompany the lack of a fresh water source, the citizens of 'Akka were as harsh as their surroundings.

The exiles, men, women, and children, were taken to a barracks within the city. Baha'u'llah's daughter recalled the ordeal,

> When we had entered the barracks the massive door was closed upon us and the great iron bolts thrown home. I cannot find words to describe the filth and stench of that

vile place. We were nearly up to our ankles in mud in the room into which we were led. The damp, close air and the excretions of the soldiers combined to produce horrible odors. Then, being unable to bear more, I fainted. As I fainted, those about me caught me before I fell; but because of the mud and filth there was no place upon which I could be laid. On one side of the room was a man weaving a mat for the soldiers. One of our friends took this mat and I was placed upon it. Then they begged for water, but they could not get it. The soldiers would permit no one to go out. There was a pool of water on the dirt floor, in which the mat-maker had been moistening his rushes. Some of this water was dipped up and strained and put to my lips. I swallowed a little and revived; but the water was so foul that my stomach rejected it, and I fainted again.[5]

Baha'u'llah was placed in a cell by himself. Most of the other exiles were crowded into another cell. 'Abdu'l-Baha found a place in the basement in a room that had formerly been used as a morgue. The effects of the humid, putrid air in the room remained with him the rest of his life. On the first night, Baha'u'llah and the exiles were denied food and water. The only water available to them was in a small pool that had previously been used for washing. There were several nursing mothers among the exiles. Due to dehydration, they had no milk for the babies. Children were heard crying and begging for food throughout the night.

The next day, each exile was given water and gritty

rice that a few of them managed to eat. One of the friends found among his baggage some dried bread. They made a dish with this bread and sent it to Baha'u'llah, who was very ill. Baha'u'llah ordered the friends to give the food to the children. Food continued to be scarce in the days that followed. Whenever there was a shortage, Baha'u'llah would eat only bread and insist that his food be given to the children.

Almost all of the exiles became ill with malaria, dysentery or typhoid. One of those who did not initially fall ill was 'Abdu'l-Baha, who day and night cared for his sick companions. The guards did not allow a doctor to be called, so 'Abdu'l-Baha used some quinine and bismuth he had brought to treat the illnesses, prepared broth and rice for the ill, and provided comfort. Three of the exiles died soon after their arrival. There was no money to provide for their burial. Baha'u'llah gave his one remaining possession, a small carpet, to the guards in exchange for a proper burial. It was later discovered that the guards had not fulfilled their end of the agreement and had buried the bodies without coffins, dressed in their clothes instead of the customary white winding sheets.

The guards quickly came to admire 'Abdu'l-Baha. They had never seen anyone care for others so devotedly, without regard for his own rest or comfort. Eventually, the long weeks of caring for his companions caused 'Abdu'l-Baha to fall ill as well. The guards were so moved by his self-sacrificing actions that they allowed a physician to come and attend to 'Abdu'l-Baha, and he soon recovered.

This fourth exile of Baha'u'llah, like previous exiles, did not diminish the flow of his writings. As he once wrote, "Never will the barking of dogs deter the Nightingale from warbling its melodies."[6] During the exile and upon his arrival in 'Akka, Baha'u'llah continued his series of tablets to kings and rulers that began in Adrianople. In some of them he recounts the sufferings imposed on his followers, and in particular, questions the appropriateness of placing such hardships on the women and children exiled with him. He reminds them that the only crime for which he and his followers have been found guilty is the crime of starting a new religion. If the reasoning here, Baha'u'llah suggests, is that religions which are ancient are to be preferred, then why are his Muslim persecutors not following the Old or New Testaments?

If his crime, Baha'u'llah continues, is that he has founded a new religion, then before him Muhammad committed the same crime, and before him, Christ and Moses as well. Baha'u'llah goes on to promise that the persecution of his Faith will not hinder its progress, for "Adversity is the oil which feedeth the flame of this Lamp and by which its light is increased. . . ."[7] In his letter to the Ottoman Sultan, Baha'u'llah condemned the abuses of civil power committed by the Ottoman Prime Minister against the Baha'is. Baha'u'llah warned them of the spiritual consequences of being seduced by power in retelling a classic tale from a poem by Sana'i in which a man awoke from a night of drunkenness and was horrified to discover that he had spent the night, not as he had imagined, but in the embrace of a dog!

SHORTLY AFTER THE EXILES ARRIVED IN 'AKKA, the decree of Sultan Aziz was read in the mosque to warn the people against associating in any way with the Baha'is. This decree declared that Baha'u'llah was one who would lead the people astray and was to be incarcerated for the rest of his life. He and the other exiles were not allowed to associate either with each other or the citizens of 'Akka. This decree prejudiced the minds of the people against the Baha'is.

The exiles were gradually placed in various rooms in the barracks. 'Abdu'l-Baha hired a man to come to the barracks and teach them how to weave rush mats. They could then take these to the market and sell them to provide for themselves some additional food and other necessities.

Eventually, the guards came to trust 'Abdu'l-Baha enough to let him and a few of the exiles go to the market each day to get provisions. One of the religious leaders of 'Akka, Shaykh Mahmud, rudely confronted 'Abdu'l-Baha one day in the market. The kindly response of 'Abdu'l-Baha to the shaykh caused him to see that 'Abdu'l-Baha was a man of integrity and gentleness. And yet, he continued to be angry at the presence of the Baha'is in 'Akka. As a religious leader, he decided that he should defend the honor of his faith and his city by killing Baha'u'llah. He approached the barracks and because he was an important man, the guards let him enter. The guards announced the presence of the shaykh to Baha'u'llah and asked him if he wished to see him. Baha'u'llah responded that he should first put away his weapon. The shaykh was surprised at this, since his weapon was hidden inside his cloak and not even the guards had suspected his plan. He immediately left the barracks.

Later he decided that what had happened was a coincidence. He was, after all, a strong man and could kill Baha'u'llah with his bare hands if he wanted to. He went back to the barracks and when the guards announced him, this time Baha'u'llah said the shaykh should first cleanse his heart. The shaykh was doubly astonished this time and left again. The third time he went to the barracks, his motivation was curiosity to know more about Baha'u'llah. This time Baha'u'llah invited him into his cell. They talked for long hours and the shakyh became a friend and supporter of Baha'u'llah. The shaykh would even leave the city at night to meet with the Baha'is who had been unable to enter the city. In the cover of night, they would pretend to be his lantern-carriers and in this way he was able to bring a few of them into the city. Most of the Baha'is who tried to enter 'Akka during the day were spotted at the city gates and turned away.

THE FAMILY OF BAHA'U'LLAH felt sorry for the many believers who had traveled so far under such difficult and dangerous circumstances to see Baha'u'llah, only to be turned away by the guards so near their goal. Soon, however, the family was plunged into a much deeper sorrow as the twenty-three-year-old younger brother of 'Abdu'l-Baha, Mihdi, was killed in an accident. Mihdi had been left behind on Baha'u'llah's first exile to Baghdad. He had been taken to the family later in Baghdad and had been with them through all of the further exiles. Mihdi was a young man of intense purity. One evening, he was pacing back and forth on the roof of the barracks, absorbed in prayer, when he fell through an open skylight onto a wooden crate that pierced his ribs. These injuries resulted in his death, twenty-two hours later. Before he died, Mihdi had one final prayer with his grieving father beside him. He asked that God make of his life a ransom for those Baha'is who traveled from great distances and were unable to see Baha'u'llah. Of this tremendous sacrifice Baha'u'llah wrote, "I have, O my Lord, offered up that which Thou hast given Me, that Thy servants may be quickened, and all that dwell on earth be united."[8]

Shortly after the death of Mihdi, Turkish troops were mobilized in 'Akka, making it necessary to move the exiles to other quarters to make room for the troops in the barracks. The exiles were placed in a house in 'Akka. This less restrictive location provided greater opportunities for Baha'is to meet with Baha'u'llah. In this way, the dying prayer of Mihdi was answered.

Some of the houses in which other exiles were placed were too small for the number of residents sent there. In one home, more than a dozen people had to sleep packed shoulder to shoulder on the floor of a small room. One of the Baha'is preferred to sleep on a shelf in the room until one night he rolled off in his sleep on top of his sleeping companions. Other Baha'is, including 'Abdu'l-Baha, were placed in a caravanserai with a leaky roof and a booming flea population. 'Abdu'l-Baha took the smallest room for himself and slept on a sheepskin rug on the floor. The ever-active fleas allowed for little rest, however. 'Abdu'l-Baha discovered that if he turned the sheepskin over every hour or so, it would take the fleas a little while to find him on the other side and in this way he was able to get a little rest. Despite the crowded and uncomfortable conditions, the Baha'is were happy to be free of the barracks, especially since they now had more opportunities to be near Baha'u'llah.

ONE OF THE MOST IMPORTANT BOOKS written by Baha'ullah in 'Akka was the Kitab-i Aqdas (Most Holy Book). Written around 1873, it is essentially a book of laws and spiritual teachings. In citing the need for religious law, Baha'u'llah writes, "They whom God hath endued with insight will readily recognize that the precepts laid down by God constitute the highest means for the maintenance of order in the world and the security of its peoples."9

The Kitab-i Aqdas contains guidance for the spiritual life of the individual Baha'i such as prayer, fasting, marriage, the education of children, and ethical teachings. It also creates the features of Baha'i community life such as the holding of periodic meetings, and the building of houses of worship with associated charitable trusts such as orphanages and homes for the aged. In the Kitab-i Aqdas, Baha'u'llah outlines the administrative institutions of the Baha'i Faith, which are elected bodies, while at the same time abolishing the institution of priesthood; in his social teachings he abolishes slavery, encourages charitable funds, exalts work to the rank of worship, enjoins his followers to associate with followers of all faiths in a spirit of friendliness, warns against fanaticism and bigotry, and calls upon all people to abandon whatever ideologies have caused them to shun one another.

Some of these laws were designed to be gradually implemented among Baha'is; others are designed for a future time envisioned by Baha'u'llah when mankind becomes tired of the spiritual dearth of materialism, governments become threatened by the consequences of unrestrained nationalism, and people begin to seek spiritual solutions to the problems of the world. Using the metaphor of wine to describe the ecstasy of a soul intoxicated by the love of God, Baha'u'llah said of this book:

> Think not that We have revealed unto you a mere code of laws. Nay, rather, We have unsealed the choice Wine with the fingers of might and power.[10]

Other writings of Baha'u'llah, written in his later years, address the needs of humanity as a whole. The most important need that Baha'u'llah identified was for unity: "Ye are all the leaves of one tree and the drops of one ocean."[11] This is a step beyond the Golden Rule.

The Golden Rule, which is found in all the major religions, teaches us to treat others as we would like to be treated. Baha'u'llah calls us to a higher understanding that we are all part of one reality. When we harm others, we are harming ourselves. Baha'u'llah compared the human race to the human body. If one part of the body is afflicted, for example, the entire body is threatened. This awareness links unity and peace with justice. In the words of Baha'u'llah:

> The light of men is Justice. Quench it not with the contrary winds of oppression and tyranny. The purpose of justice is the appearance of unity among men.[12]

Nonetheless, Baha'u'llah remained a prisoner, under house arrest, in the city of 'Akka, in a remote area of northern Palestine. His followers were few and his writings unpublished. It appeared that his message was almost unheard. A combination of government oppression and religious fanaticism had almost silenced him.

But very suddenly, even miraculously, that would all change.

BAHA'U'LLAH'S RESIDENCE AT BAHJI

CHAPTER 6

The Country: A Devotion Kings Might Envy

> That all nations should become one in faith and all men as brothers; that the bonds of affection and unity between the sons of men should be strengthened; that diversity of religion should cease, and differences of race be annulled—what harm is there in this?
>
> —Baha'u'llah[1]

ONE DAY IN THE PRISON CITY of 'Akka, Baha'u'llah mentioned to 'Abdu'l-Baha, "I have not gazed on verdure for nine years. The country is the world of the soul, the city is the world of bodies."[2] 'Abdu'l-Baha immediately set his heart on finding a new place for Baha'u'llah to live. There was a Pasha in 'Akka who owned an estate called Mazra'ih about four miles north of 'Akka. The Pasha was elderly and no longer cared to visit his estate in the country. 'Abdu'l-Baha arranged to rent the estate from the Pasha at a reasonable rate. He hired some men to make some minor repairs to it.

When the estate was ready, 'Abdu'l-Baha decided to inspect the work. Although he was officially a prisoner not allowed to leave 'Akka, 'Abdu'l-Baha walked through the city gates, past the guards who did not stop him, and went on to Mazra'ih. 'Abdu'l-Baha next arranged for a banquet and invited the officials of 'Akka. At the banquet, he announced his intention to bring his father to this house.

'Abdu'l-Baha then tried to persuade Baha'u'llah to visit Mazra'ih. No matter how he insisted, Baha'u'llah would always respond, "I am a prisoner." 'Abdu'l-Baha had prominent officials of 'Akka go to Baha'u'llah and personally invite him to leave the city and live at Mazra'ih. Again Baha'u'llah responded, "I am a prisoner." One shaykh replied, "God forbid! Who has the power to make you a prisoner? . . . I beg you to come out and go to the palace. It is beautiful and verdant. The trees are lovely, and the oranges like balls of fire!"[3]

After much imploring, Baha'u'llah finally consented to go. After nine years, Baha'u'llah was free to enjoy the beauty of nature at Mazra'ih. The estate had a stream, a grove of pine trees, and adjoined a small farm.

Two years later, 'Abdu'l-Baha acquired a home that had been vacated by a Pasha during an earlier epidemic. Baha'u'llah lived there at the mansion of Bahji for the remainder of his life. Although Baha'u'llah was still officially a prisoner, the decree of Sultan Aziz was in reality a dead letter. No official of 'Akka cared to enforce it. Baha'u'llah now moved about as he pleased. Some days he was at Bahji, some days he went to the farm at Mazra'ih, occasionally he pitched his tent on Mount Carmel near Haifa. 'Abdu'l-Baha wrote that the rulers of Palestine envied the respect he received. Many officials requested meetings with him, but he seldom granted interviews with government officials by this time.

'Abdu'l-Baha tells one such story:

> One day the government leaders, pillars of the country, the city's ulamas, leading mystics and intellectuals came out to the Mansion. The Blessed Beauty [Baha'u'llah] paid them no attention whatever. They were not admitted to His presence, nor did He inquire after any of them. I sat down with them and kept them company for some hours, after which they returned whence they had come. Although the royal [command] specifically decreed that Baha'u'llah was to be held in solitary confinement within the 'Akka fortress, in a cell, under perpetual guard; that He was never to set foot outside; that He was never even to see any of the believers—notwithstanding such a farman, such a drastic order, His tent was raised in majesty on the heights of Mount Carmel. What greater display of power could there be than this.[4]

Baha'u'llah and the members of his family had lived in dignity and resignation during the hardship of their exiles. Now with the influx of Baha'is from Persia came funds that were donated to Baha'u'llah. Deprivation was now superceded by detachment. As the lives of Baha'u'llah and his family showed how the spirit can rise above poverty, they now showed how the same spirit can rise above material concerns during relative prosperity. The members of the household continued to live in the utmost simplicity. They used the gifts and funds they were given to mitigate the hardships of the poor and to cheer the hearts of the friends for whom even the simplest gifts of tea or sugar from the hand of Baha'u'llah were priceless treasures.

Baha'u'llah taught his followers to rely on God, not on the transitory things of the world, such as money and prestige that can be yours one day, and gone the next. From his Hidden Words:

> Be not troubled in poverty nor confident in riches, for poverty is followed by riches, and riches are followed by poverty. Yet to be poor in all save God is a wondrous gift . . .[5]

In one of his letters to the shah, Baha'u'llah recalls an event from his childhood that spoke to him of the transitory nature of material concerns. At the wedding of a relative, he witnessed a spectacular and elaborate puppet show about a king and his fawning court outfitted with ornate costumes, pageantry, the smoke from a round of volleys, and the fanfare of trumpets. Later Baha'u'llah encountered a man with a box leaving the wedding.

Baha'u'llah asked the man what was in the box. The man replied that all the lavish trappings of the king and his entourage, their pomp and glory were now contained within that box. Baha'u'llah stated that ever since that day, all the vanities of the world seemed to him as insignificant as the trappings put away in that puppeteer's box.

DURING THE LATER YEARS of Baha'u'llah's life, 'Abdu'l-Baha attended to all worldly matters so that Baha'u'llah was free to write and meet with his followers. If compiled, the teachings of Baha'u'llah would amount to well over one-hundred volumes. The amanuensis of Baha'u'llah, Mirza Aqa Jan, had a particularly rapid method of taking dictation that came to be called "revelation writing." Practically no one but Mirza Aqa Jan could read this writing. He would sit near Baha'u'llah with a large bowl of ink, a stack of papers, and ten or twelve reed pens. His pen jumped rapidly across the papers, making a shrill sound that accompanied the voice of Baha'u'llah. As he paced back and forth in his room, Baha'u'llah would often chant his writings or speak them, depending upon the theme.

> Blessed is he whom His Call hath attracted to the summit of glory . . . and who hath recognized through the shrill voice of My Pen of Glory that which the Lord of this world and of the next hath willed.
> —Baha'u'llah[6]

Mirza Aqa Jan's pen would occasionally slip from his hand, and he quickly would grasp another and continue. After he took dictation, he would go over the notes with Baha'u'llah, who would correct any inaccuracies or errors. These would then be read aloud to several persons who would transcribe them.

These transcriptions were disseminated throughout Persia and called into being a new community that was radically at odds with the prevailing culture. Baha'is began to use democratic principles of equity and consultation while their nation's government was jointly ruled by a monarch and ayatollahs. Baha'i women were greatly restricted by the customs and laws of their country but still managed to have important roles in the development of the Baha'i community. Additional sources of inspiration to the developing Baha'i community were Baha'is who traveled to 'Akka and returned to Persia eager to share their vision of the teachings of Baha'u'llah.

BAHA'U'LLAH WOULD OCCASIONALLY take a respite from writing to spend time with members of the extended family as well as Baha'is who came to Bahji to visit him. Often there would be picnics in the refreshing gardens at Bahji where Baha'u'llah would pay particular attention to the children. He praised them for their good conduct and cleanliness, listened to the details of their lives, and rewarded them with special sweets. To all of them he was as a loving father. One Baha'i wrote in his memoirs that as a young child, he and his family would go to Bahji and meet with Baha'u'llah on Fridays. Typically the friends would gather in a downstairs room waiting for Baha'u'llah. One day when he was five years old, he wandered about the mansion and unbeknownst to his parents, wandered upstairs. He found a room where grocery staples were kept and among them was a large bag of sugar. On impulse he plunged his hand into the sugar and gulped down a handful. Suddenly he was aware of footsteps behind him. It was Baha'u'llah! Slowly and gently Baha'u'llah approached the boy and looked down at his hands. He then took the boy by the hand and walked him over to a tray of sweets. Offering him some candy, Baha'u'llah lovingly smiled at him and said, "It seems that you like sweets."

THE FINAL SIGNIFICANT WORK written in the closing years of Baha'u'llah's life is the Epistle to the Son of the Wolf. This book, which has been translated into English, was written to the son of an Islamic cleric who had ordered the execution of two wealthy Baha'is in Isfahan. These two brothers, Hasan and Husayn, were merchants in Isfahan, respected equally for their wealth, their philanthropy, and their personal integrity. The cleric ordered their execution on the official grounds that they were Baha'is. He had other motives as well. He owed the brothers a very large amount of money. If they were executed, not only would he be free from the debt but also would be able to confiscate their wealth for himself.

On the day of their execution, Hasan and Husayn stood arm in arm with great composure and serenity. It is important to note that these two men did not wish to die. As with the thousands of other Baha'i martyrs of their time, they had families that they loved and did not wish to leave. They enjoyed their lives, and had much to live for. Their lives had great meaning to them and to those around them because they lived to serve humanity. Yet when they were given the choice to recant their faith or choose death, they chose to die as Baha'is rather than to live without the honor of being Baha'is. How could they live without the very Faith that sustained them? Just as the proof of the existence of a Creator is creation itself, the evidence of the power of Baha'u'llah is the new creation he called into being, a new race of human beings that places the promptings of the soul above all else.

Baha'u'llah called for the abolition of the institution of priesthood in part because mankind has reached a stage of maturity when people can read the word of God for themselves and let it take root and flourish

> O Son of Man!
> My eternity is My creation, I have created it for thee. Make it the garment of thy temple ... clothe thyself therewith, that thou mayest be to all eternity the revelation of My everlasting being.
> —Baha'u'llah[7]

in their lives. Baha'u'llah referred to corrupt clerics like the one who issued the death warrant against Hasan and Husayn as "the last trace of sunlight upon the mountaintop."[8] He warned him that soon he and his kind would fade away and be no more. To the cleric, Baha'u'llah wrote, "Thinkest thou that thou wilt consume that which thine iniquity hath amassed? Nay . . . . The things thou possessest shall profit thee not, nor what thou hast laid up through thy cruelty. . . ."[9]

The cleric made a series of political blunders that left him penniless and banished from Isfahan. Eventually he was allowed to return to the city, where he died a horrible death. He is believed to have contracted cancer of the throat. He had an enormous abscess on his neck. It gave him excruciating pain in his last days and emitted such a foul odor that his wife and daughter could barely stand to take care of him. It was widely known that at the time of the execution of Hasan and Husayn, in response to those who questioned the justice of putting these two to death, the cleric had placed his hands on his own neck and said, "If there be any sin in this let it be upon my neck!"[10]

SHRINE OF BAHA'U'LLAH
The final resting place of the Prophet-Founder of the Baha'i Faith.

CHAPTER 7

Final Passage:
A Vision for the Ages

Let not your hearts be perturbed . . . In My presence amongst you there is a wisdom, and in My absence there is yet another, inscrutable to all but God . . .
—Baha'u'llah[1]

IN APRIL OF 1890, Edward Granville Browne, a professor from Cambridge, visited Baha'u'llah at Bahji. E. G. Browne was fluent in the Persian language, was completely in love with Persian literature and culture, and traveled a great deal throughout Persia. He wrote extensively about the early Babi movement. He once remarked that if a historian living at the time of Christ had been aware of the importance of the unfolding movement and had chronicled its progress, what a gift to humanity that would have been. He considered the Babi movement to have such long-ranging and worldwide significance that he devoted most of his career to study of the movement.

Browne has given us a compelling description of his meeting with Baha'u'llah:

> The face of him on whom I gazed I can never forget, though I cannot describe it. Those piercing eyes seemed to read one's very soul; power and authority sat on that ample brow; while the deep lines on the forehead and face implied an age which the jet-black hair and beard flowing down in indistinguishable luxuriance almost to the waist seemed to belie. No need to ask in whose presence I stood, as I bowed myself before one who is the object of a devotion and love which kings might envy and emperors sigh for in vain!
>
> A mild dignified voice bade me be seated, and then continued:—"Praise be to God that thou hast attained! . . . Thou hast come to see a prisoner and an exile . . . . We desire but the good of the world and the happiness of the nations; yet they deem us a stirrer-up of strife and sedition worthy of bondage and banishment. . . . That all nations should become one in faith and all men as brothers; that the bonds of affection and unity between the sons of men should be strengthened; that diversity of religion should cease, and differences of race be annulled—what harm is there in this? . . . Yet so it shall be; these fruitless strifes, these ruinous wars shall pass away, and the 'Most Great Peace' shall come. . . . Do not you in Europe need this also? Is not this that which Christ foretold? . . . Yet do we see your kings and rulers lavishing their treasures more

freely on means for the destruction of the human race than on that which would conduce to the happiness of mankind. . . . These strifes and this bloodshed and discord must cease, and all men be as one kindred and one family. . . . Let not a man glory in this, that he loves his country; let him rather glory in this, that he loves his kind. . . ."

Such, so far as I can recall, were the words which, besides many others, I heard from [Baha'u'llah]. Let those who read them consider well with themselves whether such doctrines merit death and bonds, and whether the world is more likely to gain or lose by their diffusion.[2]

MAY 29, 1892, MARKED THE END of the earthly life of Baha'u'llah. Nine months earlier he had expressed his desire to leave this world. These remarks to his family helped prepare them for the end of his life. On the 8th of May he contracted a fever. The fever came and went for the following twenty-one days. During that time, he sent word to his followers through 'Abdu'l-Baha that: "All the friends must remain patient and steadfast, and arise for the promotion of the Cause of God. They should not become perturbed because I shall always be with them, and will remember and care for them."[3]

Six days before he passed away, Baha'u'llah called the believers to his side. In that bittersweet encounter, he praised them all for their steadfastness and prayed that God would enable them to remain united after his passing. One believer by the name of Isma'il recalled that at his last meeting with Baha'u'llah, Isma'il could not stop weeping. Baha'u'llah drew him near, and taking Isma'il's handkerchief from him, wiped the tears from his eyes.

Eight hours after sunset on May 29, 1892, Baha'u'llah's wish to leave this world was granted as his eyes closed for the last time. Eyes that had seen countless sorrows, and yet continued to see. Eyes that witnessed love and betrayal, bounty and poverty. Eyes that envisioned what could be and humanity's disbelief that glory was within its reach. Eyes in which all seekers found compassion, forgiveness, inspiration. Eyes that could see into the depths of an enemy and love him anyway. Eyes that envisioned a higher path for humanity, and envisioned this through the darkness of the black pit, through the bars of his cell in 'Akka, through the limitations of his time and his cultural background.

And his vision is still with us. We find it in his vast and beautiful writings. We can begin to see it in the Baha'i communities all around the planet that bear his name.

PART
Two

Baha'i Principles

*The fundamental purpose
animating the Faith of God and His Religion
is to safeguard the interests
and promote the unity
of the human race,
and to foster the spirit of love
and fellowship amongst men.*

—Baha'u'llah[1]

'ABDU'L-BAHA, THE SON OF BAHA'U'LLAH, c. 1912

CHAPTER 8

Transition and Succession

> *My object is none other than the betterment of the world and the tranquillity of its peoples. The well-being of mankind, its peace and security, are unattainable unless and until its unity is firmly established.*
>
> —Baha'u'llah[2]

SINCE THE PASSING OF BAHA'U'LLAH, the Baha'i Faith has spread to every nation on the globe and has attracted over five-million adherents. The Baha'is are composed of every race, culture and class—highly diverse yet united in their work to bring about a change in the hearts and minds of humanity.

The Baha'i Faith has been protected from the schisms and divisions that have plagued religions of the past by the provisions Baha'u'llah outlined for his

Covenant. After his passing, leadership passed to his eldest son 'Abdu'l-Baha, whom Baha'u'llah designated as the authorized interpreter of his teachings and a model of Baha'i life. 'Abdu'l-Baha explained his father's Covenant with the Baha'is in these words:

> Inasmuch as great differences and divergences of denominational belief had arisen throughout the past, every man with a new idea attributing it to God, Baha'u'llah desired that there should not be any ground or reason for disagreement among the Baha'is. Therefore with His Own Pen He wrote the Book of His Covenant, addressing His relations and all people of the world, saying: "Verily, I have appointed One Who is the Center of My Covenant. All must obey Him; all must turn to Him; He is the expounder of My Book and He is informed of My purpose. All must turn to Him. Whatsoever He says is correct, for verily He knoweth the texts of My Book. Other than He, no one doth know My Book." The purpose of this statement is that there should never be discord and divergence among the Baha'is but that they should always be unified and agreed.[3]

Despite having grown up suffering the hardships of exile and prison with his father, 'Abdu'l-Baha knew great joy and displayed great kindness. The revolution of the Young Turks in 1908, finally resulted in his release from 'Akka, ending his nearly life-long imprisonment. From 1911 to 1913, he made visits to early Baha'is in Europe and America. During his travels to the West, he was asked to speak in countless churches, synagogues, meeting halls, and private homes. 'Abdu'l-Baha used these occasions to plead for world peace and to warn of the dangers of the coming World War. It is typical of his character that when asked, during his visit to America, how he could be happy despite all he had suffered and witnessed, he replied that the only prison that can harm one is "the prison of self."

After the passing of 'Abdu'l-Baha, his grandson Shoghi Effendi was named the Guardian of the Baha'i Faith. Shoghi Effendi translated many of the writings of Baha'u'llah into English. He directed the implementation of the administrative system outlined by Baha'u'llah that governs the Baha'i Faith today. This system consists of nine-member councils elected by local and national Baha'i communities. At the head of the system is the nine-member Universal House of Justice, another elected body that oversees the international affairs of the Faith.

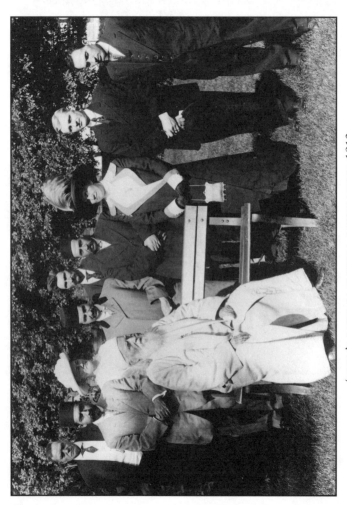

'ABDU'L-BAHÁ IN AMERICA. MINNEAPOLIS, 1912

CHAPTER 9

Social Principles

O humankind! Verily, ye are all the leaves and fruits of one tree; ye are all one. Therefore, associate in friendship; love one another; abandon prejudices of race; dispel forever this gloomy darkness of human ignorance, for the century of light, the Sun of Reality hath appeared.

—Baha'u'llah[1]

DURING HIS TRAVELS in Europe and North America on the eve of the First World War, 'Abdu'l-Baha presented the Baha'i teachings to the public on unnumbered occasions. In an effort to summarize the social teachings of Baha'u'llah, he gave the following principles as the essence of the Baha'i Message:

- Unity of Humankind
- Individual Search for Truth
- Unity of All Religions
- Harmony of Science and Religion
- Universal Education
- Equality of Women and Men
- Elimination of Prejudices of All Kinds
- Elimination of Extremes of Wealth and Poverty
- Universal Auxiliary Language
- Universal Peace Upheld by World Law

 ## Unity of Humankind

THE FIRST TEACHING OF BAHA'U'LLAH is the oneness of the human race. This is the foundation of all other Baha'i teachings. Baha'u'llah insisted that until the principle of the unity of humanity is recognized and respected, the well being of the planet cannot be secured. He wrote:

> O well-beloved ones! The tabernacle of unity hath been raised; regard ye not one another as strangers. Ye are the fruits of one tree, and the leaves of one branch.[2]

And 'Abdu'l-Baha further explained his father's teaching:

[Baha'u'llah] addressed humanity, saying: "O humankind! Verily, ye are all the leaves and fruits of one tree; ye are all one. Therefore, associate in friendship; love one another; abandon prejudices of race; dispel forever this gloomy darkness of human ignorance, for the century of light, the Sun of Reality hath appeared. Now is the time for affiliation, and now is the period of unity and concord. For thousands of years ye have been contending in warfare and strife. It is enough. Now is the time for unity. Lay aside all self-purposes, and know for a certainty that all men are the servants of one God Who will bind them together in love and agreement."[3]

 Individual Search for Truth

INDEPENDENT INVESTIGATION OF TRUTH is essential for bringing about a change towards unity. Baha'u'llah encouraged his followers to become seekers after truth. In the Hidden Words he wrote:

> The best beloved of all things in My sight is Justice; turn not away therefrom if thou desirest Me, and neglect it not that I may confide in thee. By its aid thou shalt see with thine own eyes and not through the eyes of others, and shalt know of thine own knowledge and not through the knowledge of thy neighbor.[4]

'Abdu'l-Baha said that, "blind imitation of the past will stunt the mind. But once every soul inquireth into truth, society will be freed from the darkness of continually repeating the past."[5] He also challenged us to use our God-given powers of reason:

> Furthermore, know ye that God has created in man the power of reason, whereby man is enabled to investigate reality. God has not intended man to imitate blindly his fathers and ancestors. He has endowed him with mind, or the faculty of reasoning, by the exercise of which he is to investigate and discover the truth, and that which he finds real and true he must accept. He must not be an imitator or blind follower of any soul. He must not rely implicitly upon the opinion of any man without investigation; nay, each soul must seek intelligently and independently, arriving at a real conclusion and bound only by that reality. The greatest cause of bereavement and disheartening in the world of humanity is ignorance based upon blind imitation. It is due to this that wars and battles prevail; from this cause hatred and animosity arise continually among mankind.[6]

 ## Unity of All Religions

THE BAHA'I FAITH makes no claim to be the "only true religion." No one religion can have a monopoly on the truth. Baha'u'llah envisions the great prophets, not as competitors, not even as promoters of separate religions, but rather as teachers in the same divine school of religion. They were all sent by God:

> These principles and laws, these firmly-established and mighty systems, have proceeded from one Source, and are rays of one Light. That they differ one from another is to be attributed to the varying requirements of the ages in which they were promulgated.[7]

'Abdu'l-Baha said that religion that causes people to hate one another is not a true religion:

> Religion should unite all hearts and cause wars and disputes to vanish from the face of the earth, give birth to spirituality, and bring life and light to each heart. If religion becomes a cause of dislike, hatred and division, it were better to be without it, and to withdraw from such a religion would be a truly religious act. For it is clear that the purpose of a remedy is to cure; but if the remedy should only aggravate the complaint it had better be left alone. Any religion which is not a cause of love and unity is no religion. All the holy prophets were as doctors to the soul; they gave prescriptions for the healing of mankind; thus any remedy that causes disease does not come from the great and supreme Physician.[8]

Universal Education

BAHA'U'LLAH TAUGHT the importance of recognizing our unlimited human potential:

Regard man as a mine rich in gems of inestimable value. Education can, alone, cause it to reveal its treasures, and enable mankind to benefit therefrom.[9]

'Abdu'l-Baha taught that all children must be educated equally. He spoke of universal education as one of the laws of this age:

> Baha'u'llah has announced that inasmuch as ignorance and lack of education are barriers of separation among mankind, all must receive training and instruction. Through this provision the lack of mutual understanding will be remedied and the unity of mankind furthered and advanced. Universal education is a universal law. It is, therefore, incumbent upon every father to teach and instruct his children according to his possibilities. If he is unable to educate them, the body politic, the representative of the people, must provide the means for their education.[10]

 ## Harmony of Science and Religion

THE BAHA'I WRITINGS STATE that true religion and science do not contradict each other. 'Abdu'l-Baha said that:

> We may think of science as one wing and religion as the other; a bird needs two wings for flight, one alone would be useless. Any religion that contradicts science or that is opposed to it, is only ignorance—for ignorance is the opposite of knowledge.

Religion which consists only of rites and ceremonies of prejudice is not the truth. Let us earnestly endeavor to be the means of uniting religion and science. . . .

Whatever the intelligence of man cannot understand, religion ought not to accept. Religion and science walk hand in hand, and any religion contrary to science is not the truth.[11]

During his travels in the West, 'Abdu'l-Baha warned:

Religion must reconcile and be in harmony with science and reason. If the religious beliefs of mankind are contrary to science and opposed to reason, they are none other than superstitions and without divine authority, for the Lord God has endowed man with the faculty of reason in order that through its exercise he may arrive at the verities of existence. Reason is the discoverer of the realities of things, and that which conflicts with its conclusions is the product of human fancy and imagination.[12]

 Equality of Women and Men

BAHA'U'LLAH'S TEACHINGS ON THE EQUALITY of men and women were remarkable for the time and place they were proclaimed. He wrote: "Women and men have been and will always be equal in the sight of God."[13] This proclamation made by Baha'u'llah in the nineteenth century is gradually coming to be accepted by the generality of humanity.

'Abdu'l-Baha emphasized this teaching during his travels in Europe and America. He said:

> In proclaiming the oneness of mankind [Baha'u'llah] taught that men and women are equal in the sight of God and that there is no distinction to be made between them. The only difference between them now is due to lack of education and training. . . . The world of humanity has two wings, as it were: One is the female; the other is the male. If one wing be defective, the strong perfect wing will not be capable of flight. The world of humanity has two hands. If one be imperfect, the capable hand is restricted and unable to perform its duties. God is the Creator of mankind. He has endowed both sexes with perfections and intelligence, given them physical members and organs of sense, without differentiation or distinction as to superiority; therefore, why should woman be considered inferior? This is not according to the plan and justice of God. He has created them equal; in His estimate there is no question of sex.[14]

Elimination of Prejudice

PREJUDICES OF RACE, religion, gender and nationality have been the root cause of oppression and war through all of history. The Baha'i writings regard these prejudices as superstitions representative of an immature stage of human progress. In his writings, Baha'u'llah called us to realize our essential unity. 'Abdu'l-Baha explained:

Sources of human dissension are political, racial and patriotic prejudices. These have been removed by Baha'u'llah. He has said, and has guarded His statement by rational proofs from the Holy Books, that the world of humanity is one race, the surface of the earth one place of residence and that these imaginary racial barriers and political boundaries are without right or foundation. Man is degraded in becoming the captive of his own illusions and suppositions. The earth is one earth, and the same atmosphere surrounds it. No difference or preference has been made by God for its human inhabitants; but man has laid the foundation of prejudice, hatred and discord with his fellowman by considering nationalities separate in importance and races different in rights and privileges.[15]

 ## Extremes of Wealth and Poverty

BAHA'U'LLAH OUTLINED a spiritual path towards the elimination of extremes of wealth and poverty. This path is a call both to the poor and to the wealthy.

Baha'u'llah elevated work done in the spirit of service to the rank of worship of God. He wrote that "the best of men are they that earn a livelihood by their calling and spend upon themselves and upon their kindred for the love of God, the Lord of all worlds."[16]

Baha'u'llah also reminded the wealthy of their opportunity to assist the poor:

O children of dust!

Tell the rich of the midnight sighing of the poor, lest heedlessness lead them into the path of destruction, and deprive them of the Tree of Wealth. To give and to be generous are attributes of Mine; well is it with him that adornest himself with My virtues.[17]

And 'Abdu'l-Baha observed:

When we see poverty allowed to reach a condition of starvation it is a sure sign that somewhere we shall find tyranny. Men must bestir themselves in this matter, and no longer delay in altering conditions which bring the misery of grinding poverty to a very large number of the people. The rich must give of their abundance, they must soften their hearts and cultivate a compassionate intelligence, taking thought for those sad ones who are suffering from lack of the very necessities of life.[18]

 ## Universal Auxiliary Language

BAHA'U'LLAH PROPOSED that every child in the world be taught an auxiliary language, so that to whatever city someone traveled, it would be as if "he were entering his own home."[19]

'Abdu'l-Baha considered this plan to be an important step toward peace:

Diversity of languages has been a fruitful cause of discord. The function of language is to convey the thought and purpose of one to another. Therefore, it matters not what language man speaks or employs. . . . Baha'u'llah advocated one language as the greatest means of unity and the basis of international conference. He wrote to the kings and rulers of the various nations, recommending that one language should be sanctioned and adopted by all governments. According to this each nation should acquire the universal language in addition to its native tongue. The world would then be in close communication, consultation would become general, and dissensions due to diversity of speech would be removed.[20]

 Universal Peace

BAHA'U'LLAH CALLED for the creation of a collective security agreement that would be ratified by all the nations of the world. In this agreement, the borders of nations would be permanently agreed upon, and all disputes regarding resources and other issues would be resolved by international arbitration.

'Abdu'l-Baha called again and again for peace among nations upheld by international law. After he spoke these words in 1912, the world would soon experience the most destructive war it had ever seen:

Universal peace will be established among the nations of the world by international agreement. The greatest catastrophe in the world of humanity today is war. Europe is a storehouse of explosives awaiting a spark. All the European nations are on edge, and a single flame will set on fire the whole of that continent. Implements of war and death are multiplied and increased to an inconceivable degree, and the burden of military maintenance is taxing the various countries beyond the point of endurance. Armies and navies devour the substance and possessions of the people; the toiling poor, the innocent and helpless are forced by taxation to provide munitions and armament for governments bent upon conquest of territory and defense against powerful rival nations. There is no greater or more woeful ordeal in the world of humanity today than impending war. Therefore, international peace is a crucial necessity. An arbitral court of justice shall be established by which international disputes are to be settled. Through this means all possibility of discord and war between the nations will be obviated.[21]

PART
Three

Teachings of Baha'u'llah

To be a Baha'i simply means to love all the world;
to love humanity, and try to serve it;
to work for universal peace
and universal brotherhood.

—'Abdu'l-Baha[1]

'ABDU'L-BAHA IN LONDON, 1911

CHAPTER 10 — *Our Spiritual Reality*

> *True loss is for him whose days have been spent in utter ignorance of his self.*
>
> —Baha'u'llah[2]

THE BIBLE STORY of creation in Genesis tells us that man was created from the elements of the earth. In his body, he is completely one with nature:

> And the Lord God formed man of the dust of the ground, and breathed into his nostrils the breath of life: and man became a living soul.[3]

Read literally, this simply tells us that God gave Adam CPR. Reading another way, we consider that breath is a symbol of spirit. This story tells us that there is something of the spirit of God within humanity. In this sense, every human being is created in the image of God, for God is Spirit. Baha'u'llah taught that the purpose of this life was to develop that spirit.

We can compare this idea of spiritual development to a child in the womb of its mother. The purpose of the fetus in that brief interval is to develop physically in preparation for this world. A child in the womb has no need for eyes, legs, lungs, or the faculties of speech. Yet all these physical capacities must come together in the womb in order for the child to reach its full potential in this world. Likewise, our purpose in this physical world is to develop spiritual attributes that we will need in the next world.

These spiritual qualities will not be fully realized in this lifetime. As Baha'u'llah explained:

> Consider, moreover, how the fruit, ere it is formed, lieth potentially within the tree. Were the tree to be cut into pieces, no sign nor any part of the fruit, however small, could be detected. When it appeareth, however, it manifesteth itself, as thou hast observed, in its wondrous beauty and glorious perfection. Certain fruits, indeed, attain their fullest development only after being severed from the tree.[4]

And in another passage Baha'u'llah explains:

> Man is like unto a tree. If he be adorned with fruit, he hath been and will ever be worthy of praise and commen-

dation. Otherwise a fruitless tree is but fit for fire. The fruits of the human tree are exquisite, highly desired and dearly cherished. Among them are upright character, virtuous deeds and a goodly utterance.[5]

HOW DO WE BEGIN to develop our spiritual fruits? Just as a tree depends upon the sun, the earth, and water for its life, our spiritual lives need external support. First and foremost, we need the love of God. As Baha'u'llah wrote:

> For every one of you his paramount duty is to choose for himself that on which no other may infringe and none usurp from him. Such a thing—and to this the Almighty is My witness—is the love of God, could ye but perceive it.[6]

Second, we need grounding in a spiritual education. Baha'u'llah described the founders of the great religions as "Roots of Knowledge." Their essential spiritual teachings give people the strength and foundation needed for character development.

Finally, the tree of our being needs to be watered with the word of God. From the writings of Baha'u'llah:

> The Water for these trees is the living water of the sacred Words uttered by the Beloved of the world. In one instant are such trees planted and in the next their branches shall, through the outpourings of the showers of divine mercy, have reached the skies.[7]

The "life-giving water" of Baha'u'llah's teachings is meant for humanity as a whole, as well as for the individual. Baha'i scriptures are concerned with individual spiritual growth but also with the protection and guidance of society. In this day, it is not only the individual soul that seeks salvation, it is the entire human race.

CHAPTER 11

Spiritual Virtues

> *O friends! Be not careless of the virtues with which ye have been endowed, neither be neglectful of your high destiny. . . . Ye are the stars of the heaven of understanding, the breeze that stirreth at the break of day, the soft-flowing waters upon which must depend the very life of all men . . . .*
>
> —Baha'u'llah[1]

SPIRITUALITY IS MORE of a path than a destination. It cannot be purchased, inherited, or passively absorbed. It requires the application of will. It is not a formula to be followed, but a tendency we must nurture within ourselves. It is a treasure unearthed after much effort. Baha'i writings assure us that within our souls are gems that may be discovered and polished through the discipline of a spiritual life.

God's relationship to humanity in its essence is the call of the Beloved to His loved ones. From the Hidden Words of Baha'u'llah:

> O Son of Man!
> I loved thy creation, hence I created thee. Wherefore, do thou love Me, that I may name thy name and fill thy soul with the spirit of life.
>
> O Son of the Wondrous Vision!
> I have breathed within thee a breath of My own Spirit, that thou mayest be My lover. Why hast thou forsaken Me and sought a beloved other than Me?
>
> O Son of Justice!
> Whither can a lover go but to the land of his beloved? and what seeker findeth rest away from his heart's desire? To the true lover reunion is life, and separation is death. His breast is void of patience and his heart hath no peace.[2]

How does God reveal His love to us? How should we respond to His love? How then should we live? Baha'u'llah taught us how in poetic passages such as this:

> Be generous in prosperity, and thankful in adversity. Be worthy of the trust of thy neighbor, and look upon him with a bright and friendly face. Be a treasure to the poor, an admonisher to the rich, an answerer to the cry of the needy, a preserver of the sanctity of thy pledge. Be fair in

thy judgment, and guarded in thy speech. Be unjust to no man, and show all meekness to all men. Be as a lamp unto them that walk in darkness, a joy to the sorrowful, a sea for the thirsty, a haven for the distressed, an upholder and defender of the victim of oppression. Let integrity and uprightness distinguish all thine acts. Be a home for the stranger, a balm to the suffering, a tower of strength for the fugitive. Be eyes to the blind, and a guiding light unto the feet of the erring. Be an ornament to the countenance of truth, a crown to the brow of fidelity, a pillar of the temple of righteousness, a breath of life to the body of mankind, an ensign of the hosts of justice, a luminary above the horizon of virtue, a dew to the soil of the human heart, an ark on the ocean of knowledge, a sun in the heaven of bounty, a gem on the diadem of wisdom, a shining light in the firmament of thy generation, a fruit upon the tree of humility. We pray God to protect thee from the heat of jealousy and the cold of hatred. He verily is nigh, ready to answer.[3]

 Prayer and Meditation

PRAYER IS CONVERSATION with God. Prayer is necessary for spiritual development because in that state we connect to a higher purpose. 'Abdu'l-Baha explained that: "The state of prayer is the best of conditions, for man is then associating with God. Prayer verily bestoweth life, particularly when offered in private and at times, such as midnight, when freed from daily cares."[4]

Prayer should be followed by meditation and meditation should be followed by action. 'Abdu'l-Baha described meditation:

> Meditation is the key for opening the doors of mysteries. In that state man abstracts himself: in that state man withdraws himself from all outside objects; in that subjective mood he is immersed in the ocean of spiritual life and can unfold the secrets of things-in-themselves... This faculty brings forth from the invisible plane the sciences and arts. Through the meditative faculty inventions are made possible, colossal undertakings are carried out; through it governments can run smoothly. Through this faculty man enters into the very Kingdom of God.[5]

 A Spiritual Life

WE LIVE IN A TIME when many people have rejected any constraints on their behavior imposed by religion. Some have done this because they no longer accept the authority of religion; others have followed this path because of disappointment that many religious leaders who have preached high standards of morality have not followed these standards themselves. Baha'u'llah encouraged his followers to accept the disciplines of a spiritual life, since to disassociate spirituality from morality will most likely result in the loss of both:

Religion is, verily, the chief instrument for the establishment of order in the world, and of tranquility amongst its peoples. The weakening of the pillars of religion hath strengthened the foolish, and emboldened them, and made them more arrogant. Verily I say: The greater the decline of religion, the more grievous the waywardness of the ungodly. This cannot but lead in the end to chaos and confusion.6

 Family Life

BAHA'U'LLAH ENCOURAGED marriage and parenthood. In fact, all of the prophets of God have examined the human condition and concluded that marriage is the ideal foundation for society. 'Abdu'l-Baha said, "The true marriage of Baha'is is this, that husband and wife should be united both physically and spiritually, that they may ever improve the spiritual life of each other, and may enjoy everlasting unity throughout all the worlds of God. This is Baha'i marriage."7

Parents are given the responsibility to provide a spiritual and material education for their children. The mother is the child's first teacher. As 'Abdu'l-Baha explained:

> Let the mothers consider that whatever concerneth the education of children is of the first importance. . . Whensoever a mother seeth that her child hath done well, let her praise and applaud him and cheer his heart;

and if the slightest undesirable trait should manifest itself, let her counsel the child and punish him, and use means based on reason, even a slight verbal chastisement should this be necessary. It is not, however, permissible to strike a child, or vilify him, for the child's character will be totally perverted if he be subjected to blows or verbal abuse.[8]

Baha'u'llah taught that if circumstances forced his followers to choose between serving him and serving their parents, they should choose to serve their parents and let that be a path leading them closer to God. The family is like a perpetual workshop in which the virtues of the spiritual life are continually practiced and refined. Family unity is achieved when parents and children are mutually devoted to each other. Family unity leads to the progress and development of the individuals within the family. 'Abdu'l-Baha once said: "If love and agreement are manifest in a single family, that family will advance, become illumined and spiritual. . . ."[9] He also wrote:

> All the virtues must be taught the family. The integrity of the family bond must be constantly considered, and the rights of the individual members must not be transgressed. The rights of the son, the father, the mother—none of them must be transgressed, none of them must be arbitrary. Just as the son has certain obligations to his father, the father, likewise, has certain obligations to his son. The mother, the sister and other members of the household have their certain prerogatives. All these rights and prerogatives must be conserved, yet the unity of the family

must be sustained. The injury of one shall be considered the injury of all; the comfort of each, the comfort of all; the honor of one, the honor of all.10

 Love

LOVE IS THE FOUNDATION of all spiritual development. 'Abdu'l-Baha said: "Until love takes possession of the heart, no other divine bounty can be revealed in it."11 He also explained the meaning of love:

Love is heaven's kindly light, the Holy Spirit's eternal breath that vivifieth the human soul. Love is the cause of God's revelation unto man, the vital bond inherent, in accordance with the divine creation, in the realities of things. Love is the one means that ensureth true felicity both in this world and the next. Love is the light that guideth in darkness, the living link that uniteth God with man, that assureth the progress of every illumined soul. Love is the most great law that ruleth this mighty and heavenly cycle, the unique power that bindeth together the divers elements of this material world, the supreme magnetic force that directeth the movements of the spheres in the celestial realms. Love revealeth with unfailing and limitless power the mysteries latent in the universe. Love is the spirit of life unto the adorned body of mankind, the establisher of true civilization in this mortal world, and the shedder of imperishable glory upon every high-aiming race and nation.12

 ## Courtesy

BAHA'U'LLAH CALLS COURTESY "the lord of all virtues." He also states:

> We, verily, have chosen courtesy, and made it the true mark of such as are nigh unto Him. Courtesy is, in truth, a raiment which fitteth all men, whether young or old.[13]

'Abdu'l-Baha says:

> So far as ye are able, ignite a candle of love in every meeting, and with tenderness rejoice and cheer ye every heart. Care for the stranger as for one of your own; show to alien souls the same loving kindness ye bestow upon your faithful friends.[14]

And again, he says:

> Beware! Beware! Lest ye offend any heart!
> Beware! Beware! Lest ye hurt any soul!
> Beware! Beware! Lest ye deal unkindly toward any person!
> Beware! Beware! Lest ye be the cause of hopelessness to any creature![15]

 ## Kindness

BAHA'U'LLAH BEGINS the Hidden Words with this verse:

O Son of Spirit!

My first counsel is this: Possess a pure, kindly and radiant heart, that thine may be a sovereignty ancient, imperishable and everlasting.[16]

In another place, Baha'u'llah writes:

All men have been created to carry forward an ever-advancing civilization. The Almighty beareth Me witness: To act like the beasts of the field is unworthy of man. Those virtues that befit his dignity are forbearance, mercy, compassion and loving-kindness towards all the peoples and kindreds of the earth.[17]

 A Sin-Covering Eye

ON NO SUBJECT are the teachings of Baha'u'llah more emphatic and uncompromising than on the requirement to abstain from fault-finding, backbiting, and gossip. In the Hidden Words, Baha'u'llah says:

O Son of Man!

Breathe not the sins of others so long as thou art thyself a sinner. Shouldst thou transgress this command, accursed wouldst thou be, and to this I bear witness.

O Son of Being!

Ascribe not to any soul that which thou wouldst not have ascribed to thee, and say not that which thou doest not. This is My command unto thee, do thou observe it.[18]

'Abdu'l-Baha tells us:

> To be silent concerning the faults of others, to pray for them, through kindness, to correct their faults.
> To look always at the good and not at the bad. If a man has ten good qualities and one bad one, to look at the ten and forget the one; and if a man has ten bad qualities and one good one, to look at the one and forget the ten.
> Never to allow ourselves to speak one unkind word about another, even though that other be our enemy.[19]

 ## Forgiveness

AS IN ALL RELIGIONS, Baha'u'llah teaches his followers to forgive the sins of others. He says:

> He should forgive the sinful, and never despise his low estate, for none knoweth what his own end shall be. How often hath a sinner, at the hour of death, attained to the essence of faith, and, quaffing the immortal draught, hath taken his flight unto the celestial Concourse![20]

And 'Abdu'l-Baha explains:

> Among the teachings of Baha'u'llah is one requiring man, under all conditions and circumstances, to be forgiving, to love his enemy and to consider an ill-wisher as a well-wisher. Not that one should consider another as an enemy

and then put up with him . . . and be forbearing toward him. This is hypocrisy and not real love. Nay, rather, you must see your enemies as friends, your ill-wishers as well-wishers and treat them accordingly. Your love and kindness must be real . . . not merely forbearance, for forbearance, if not of the heart, is hypocrisy.[21]

Again, 'Abdu'l-Baha taught:

. . . if someone oppresses, injures and wrongs another, and the wronged man retaliates, this is vengeance and is censurable. . . . No, rather he must return good for evil, and not only forgive, but also, if possible, be of service to his oppressor. This conduct is worthy of man: for what advantage does he gain by vengeance? The two actions are equivalent; if one action is reprehensible, both are reprehensible. The only difference is that one was committed first, the other later.[22]

 Fairness

BAHA'U'LLAH EMPHASIZED in his teachings the foundational position of fairness and justice:

Be fair to yourselves and to others, that the evidences of justice may be revealed, through your deeds, among Our faithful servants. Beware lest ye encroach upon the substance of your neighbor. Prove yourselves worthy of his trust and confidence in you, and withhold not from the

Spiritual Virtues

poor the gifts which the grace of God hath bestowed upon you. He, verily, shall recompense the charitable, and doubly repay them for what they have bestowed.[23]

In the Hidden Words Baha'u'llah says:

O Son of Spirit!
The best beloved of all things in My sight is Justice; turn not away therefrom if thou desirest Me, and neglect it not that I may confide in thee. By its aid thou shalt see with thine own eyes and not through the eyes of others, and shalt know of thine own knowledge and not through the knowledge of thy neighbor. Ponder this in thy heart; how it behooveth thee to be. Verily justice is My gift to thee and the sign of My loving-kindness. Set it then before thine eyes.[24]

 ## Trustworthiness

HONESTY AND TRUSTWORTHINESS are highly praised in Baha'u'llah's writings. He says:

Trustworthiness is the greatest portal leading unto the tranquility and security of the people. In truth the stability of every affair hath depended and doth depend upon it."[25]

And again:

Beautify your tongues, O people, with truthfulness, and adorn your souls with the ornament of honesty. Beware, O people, that ye deal not treacherously with any one. Be ye the trustees of God amongst His creatures, and the emblems of His generosity amidst His people. They that follow their lusts and corrupt inclinations, have erred and dissipated their efforts. They, indeed, are of the lost. Strive, O people, that your eyes may be directed towards the mercy of God, that your hearts may be attuned to His wondrous remembrance, that your souls may rest confidently upon His grace and bounty, that your feet may tread the path of His good-pleasure. Such are the counsels which I bequeath unto you. Would that ye might follow My counsels![26]

 Service

AMONG ALL VIRTUES, Baha'u'llah reserved the highest station for service. Service to others is most praiseworthy, and service to all humanity is service to God. Work, done in the spirit of service to humanity, is regarded as worship of God. Baha'u'llah declares:

> That one indeed is a man who, today, dedicateth himself to the service of the entire human race. . . . Blessed and happy is he that ariseth to promote the best interests of the peoples and kindreds of the earth.[27]

'Abdu'l-Baha insists:

> . . . all effort and exertion put forth by man from the fullness of his heart is worship, if it is prompted by the highest motives and the will to do service to humanity.

Spiritual Virtues 105

This is worship: to serve mankind and to minister to the needs of the people. Service is prayer. A physician ministering to the sick, gently, tenderly, free from prejudice and believing in the solidarity of the human race, he is giving praise.[28]

CHAPTER 12

The True Seeker

> *The true seeker hunteth naught but the object of his quest, and the lover hath no desire save union with his beloved. Nor shall the seeker reach his goal unless he sacrifice all things. That is, whatever he hath seen, and heard, and understood, all must he set at naught, that he may enter the realm of the spirit, which is the City of God.*
>
> —Baha'u'llah[1]

BAHA'U'LLAH DESCRIBED the qualities of the true seeker, one who searches for God with all of the ardor implied in such a spiritual quest:

> O My brother! When a true seeker determineth to take the step of search in the path leading unto the knowledge of the Ancient of Days, he must, before all else, cleanse his heart, which is the seat of the revelation of the inner

mysteries of God, from the obscuring dust of all acquired knowledge.... He must so cleanse his heart that no remnant of either love or hate may linger therein, lest that love blindly incline him to error, or that hate repel him away from the truth....

That seeker must, at all times, put his trust in God, must renounce the peoples of the earth, must detach himself from the world of dust, and cleave unto Him Who is the Lord of Lords. He must never seek to exalt himself above any one, must wash away from the tablet of his heart every trace of pride and vain-glory, must cling unto patience and resignation, observe silence and refrain from idle talk. For the tongue is a smoldering fire, and excess of speech a deadly poison. Material fire consumeth the body, whereas the fire of the tongue devoureth both heart and soul. The force of the former lasteth but for a time, whilst the effects of the latter endureth a century.

That seeker should, also, regard backbiting as grievous error, and keep himself aloof from its dominion, inasmuch as backbiting quencheth the light of the heart, and extinguisheth the life of the soul. He should be content with little, and be freed from all inordinate desire. He should treasure the companionship of them that have renounced the world, and regard avoidance of boastful and worldly people a precious benefit. At the dawn of every day he should commune with God, and, with all his soul, persevere in the quest of his Beloved. He should consume every wayward thought with the flame of His loving mention, and, with the swiftness of lightning, pass by all else save Him. He should succor the dispossessed, and never withhold his favor from the destitute. He should show kindness to animals, how much more unto his fellow-man, to him who is endowed with the power of utterance. He should not hesitate to offer up his life for his Beloved, nor allow the censure of the people to turn him away from the Truth. He should not wish for others that which he doth not wish for himself, nor promise that which he doth not fulfil. With all his heart he should avoid fellowship with evil-doers, and pray for the remission of their sins. He should forgive the sinful, and never despise his low estate, for none knoweth what his own end shall be. How often hath a sinner attained, at the hour of death, to the essence of faith, and, quaffing the immortal draught, hath taken his flight unto the Concourse on high! And how often hath a devout believer, at the hour of his soul's ascension, been so changed as to fall into the nethermost fire!

Our purpose in revealing these convincing and weighty utterances is to impress upon the seeker that he should regard all else beside God as transient, and count all things save Him, Who is the Object of all adoration, as utter nothingness.

These are among the attributes of the exalted, and constitute the hallmark of the spiritually-minded. They have already been mentioned in connection with the requirements of the wayfarers that tread the path of Positive Knowledge. When the detached wayfarer and sincere seeker hath fulfilled these essential conditions, then and only then can he be called a true seeker. Whensoever he hath fulfilled the conditions implied in the verse: "Whoso maketh efforts for Us," he shall enjoy the blessings conferred by the words: "In Our Ways shall We assuredly guide him."[2]

The object of the seeker's quest is, of course, union with the Creator. Baha'u'llah likened himself, as well as the other founders of the great religions, to the true Friend, because that Friend will lead us back to God:

> Worldly friends, seeking their own good, appear to love one the other, whereas the true Friend hath loved and doth love you for your own sakes; indeed He hath suffered for your guidance countless afflictions. Be not disloyal to such a Friend, nay rather hasten unto Him.[3]

This Friend will "awaken the heart, the soul, and the spirit from the slumber of negligence." Then the seeker "will find himself endowed with a new eye, a new ear, a new heart, and a new mind." This is a great blessing! As Baha'u'llah wrote,

> Blessed the slumberer who is awakened by My Breeze. Blessed the lifeless one who is quickened through My reviving breaths. . . . Blessed the distressed one who seeketh refuge beneath the shadow of My canopy. Blessed the sore athirst who hasteneth to the soft-flowing waters of My loving-kindness. Blessed the insatiate soul who casteth away his selfish desires for love of Me and taketh his place at the banquet table which I have sent down from the heaven of divine bounty for My chosen ones. Blessed the abased one who layeth fast hold on the cord of My glory; and the needy one who entereth beneath the shadow of the Tabernacle of My wealth. Blessed the ignorant one who seeketh the fountain of My knowledge; and

the heedless one who cleaveth to the cord of My remembrance. Blessed the soul that hath been raised to life through My quickening breath and hath gained admittance into My heavenly Kingdom.[4]

The Friend calls us, not only for our own sakes, not only because of God's love for us, but also that we may contribute our part in bringing about a better world:

> Incline your hearts, O people of God, unto the counsels of your true, your incomparable Friend. The Word of God may be likened unto a sapling, whose roots have been implanted in the hearts of men. It is incumbent upon you to foster its growth through the living waters of wisdom, of sanctified and holy words, so that its root may become firmly fixed and its branches may spread out as high as the heavens and beyond.
>
> O ye that dwell on earth! The distinguishing feature that marketh the preeminent character of this Supreme Revelation consisteth in that We have, on the one hand, blotted out from the pages of God's holy Book whatsoever hath been the cause of strife, of malice and mischief amongst the children of men, and have, on the other, laid down the essential prerequisites of concord, of understanding, of complete and enduring unity.[5]

The following prayer by 'Abdu'l-Baha summarizes the central Baha'i message of the precious nature and essential unity of humanity. It is a call to all of us to uplift the banner of the oneness of mankind.

O Thou kind Lord!

Thou hast created all humanity from the same stock. Thou hast decreed that all shall belong to the same household. In Thy Holy Presence they are all Thy servants, and all mankind are sheltered beneath Thy Tabernacle; all have gathered together at Thy Table of Bounty; all are illumined through the light of Thy Providence.

O God! Thou art kind to all, Thou hast provided for all, dost shelter all, conferrest life upon all. Thou hast endowed each and all with talents and faculties, and all are submerged in the Ocean of Thy Mercy.

O Thou kind Lord! Unite all. Let the religions agree and make the nations one, so that they may see each other as one family and the whole earth as one home. May they all live together in perfect harmony.

O God! Raise aloft the banner of the oneness of mankind.

O God! Establish the Most Great Peace.

Cement Thou, O God, the hearts together.

O Thou kind Father, God! Gladden our hearts through the fragrance of Thy love. Brighten our eyes through the Light of Thy Guidance. Delight our ears with the melody of Thy Word, and shelter us all in the Stronghold of Thy Providence.

Thou art the Mighty and Powerful, Thou art the Forgiving and Thou art the One Who overlooketh the shortcomings of all mankind.[6]

'ABDU'L-BAHA

CHAPTER 13

Your Spiritual Path

> *Create in me a pure heart, O my God, and renew a tranquil conscience within me, O my Hope! Through the spirit of power confirm Thou me in Thy Cause, O my Best-Beloved, and by the light of Thy glory reveal unto me Thy path, O Thou the Goal of my desire!*
>
> —Baha'u'llah[1]

THE CHOICE THAT STANDS before each of us every day of our lives is the degree to which we will live in the material world or in the spiritual world. To live for the world of the spirit is to drink from the river of everlasting life. Baha'u'llah wrote:

> O My Servant!
> Abandon not for that which perisheth an everlasting dominion, and cast not away celestial sovereignty for a worldly desire. This is the river of everlasting life that

hath flowed from the well-spring of the pen of the merciful; well is it with them that drink!

O Son of Worldliness!
Pleasant is the realm of being, wert thou to attain thereto; glorious is the domain of eternity, shouldst thou pass beyond the world of mortality; sweet is the holy ecstasy if thou drinkest of the mystic chalice from the hands of the celestial Youth. Shouldst thou attain this station, thou wouldst be freed from destruction and death, from toil and sin.[2]

If, however, we choose to live only for this temporal life, we will know the despair and futility of earthly ambitions and desires.

O Fleeting Shadow!
Pass beyond the baser stages of doubt and rise to the exalted heights of certainty. Open the eye of truth, that thou mayest behold the veilless Beauty and exclaim: Hallowed be the Lord, the most excellent of all creators![3]

To live for the sake of your soul requires the exercise of will. Every time we make a choice based on our spiritual reality we become stronger. When we take the first step toward spirituality, we will receive divine encouragement, as promised in one of the prayers of Baha'u'llah:

Thou disappointest no one who hath sought Thee, nor dost Thou keep back from Thee any one who hath desired

Thee. Ordain Thou for me what becometh the heaven of Thy generosity, and the ocean of Thy bounty.[4]

To live for the sake of our soul requires purity. We become pure by acknowledging our imperfections to our Creator, then by striving to do better. Spiritual awakening then comes as a gift of God. In a prayer, Baha'u'llah addresses God, saying:

> My God, my Adored One, my King, my Desire!
>   What tongue can voice my thanks to Thee? I was heedless, Thou didst awaken me. I had turned back from Thee, Thou didst graciously aid me to turn towards Thee. I was as one dead, Thou didst quicken me with the water of life. I was withered, Thou didst revive me with the heavenly stream of Thine utterance which hath flowed forth from the Pen of the All-Merciful.
>   O Divine Providence! All existence is begotten by Thy bounty; deprive it not of the waters of Thy generosity, neither do Thou withhold it from the ocean of Thy mercy. I beseech Thee to aid and assist me at all times and under all conditions, and seek from the heaven of Thy grace Thine ancient favor. Thou art, in truth, the Lord of bounty, and the Sovereign of the kingdom of eternity.[5]

The following prayer by 'Abdu'l-Baha is for spiritual awakening and growth. The purpose of spirituality is not just to kindle of our own souls, but to give us the strength and courage to arise and transform the world around us:

O COMPASSIONATE GOD!

Thanks be to Thee for Thou hast awakened and made me conscious. Thou hast given me a seeing eye and favored me with a hearing ear, hast led me to Thy kingdom and guided me to Thy path. Thou hast shown me the right way and caused me to enter the ark of deliverance. O God! Keep me steadfast and make me firm and staunch. Protect me from violent tests, and preserve and shelter me in the strongly fortified fortress of Thy Covenant and Testament. Thou art the Powerful. Thou art the Seeing. Thou art the Hearing.

O Thou the Compassionate God. Bestow upon me a heart which, like unto a glass, may be illumined with the light of Thy love, and confer upon me thoughts which may change this world into a rose garden through the outpourings of heavenly grace.

Thou art the Compassionate, the Merciful. Thou art the Great Beneficent God. [6]

References

Part One: The Story of Bahá'u'lláh

1. Bahá'u'lláh, *Tablets of Bahá'u'lláh Revealed After the Kitáb-i-Aqdas* (Haifa: Bahá'í World Center, 1982), p. 219.

Chapter 1: First Light: The Dawn of a New Day

2. Bahá'u'lláh, *Epistle to the Son of the Wolf* (Wilmette: Bahá'í Publishing Trust, 1979) p. 11.
3. H. M. Balyuzi, *Bahá'u'lláh The King of Glory* (Oxford: George Ronald, 1991) p. 78.
4. Bahá'u'lláh, *Kitáb-i-Íqán* (Wilmette: Bahá'í Publishing Trust, 1974) p. 61.
5. Lady Blomfield, *The Chosen Highway* (Wilmette: Bahá'í Publishing Trust, 1970) pp. 40-41.
6. David S. Ruhe, *Robe of Light* (Oxford: George Ronald, 1994) p. 48.
7. Bahá'u'lláh, *Epistle to the Son of the Wolf*, p. 22.
8. Shoghi Effendi, *God Passes By* (Wilmette: Bahá'í Publishing Trust, 1970) pp. 101-102.
9. Bahá'u'lláh, *The Hidden Words of Bahá'u'lláh*, Persian # 13 (Wilmette: Bahá'í Publishing Trust, 1971).
10. *Ecclesiastes* 11:5, Revised Standard Version.

11. Bahá'u'lláh, *Epistle to the Son of the Wolf*, pp. 11-12.
12. Ruhe, *Robe of Light*, p. 143.
13. Bahá'u'lláh, *Hidden Words*, Arabic #32.

Chapter 2: Banished: Exile to Baghdad

1. Bahá'u'lláh, *Prayers and Meditations* (Wilmette: Bahá'í Publishing Trust, 1938) p. 23.
2. Shoghi Effendi, *God Passes By*, p. 105.
3. 'Abdu'l-Bahá, *Memorials of the Faithful* (Wilmette: Bahá'í Publishing Trust, 1971) p. 192.
4. Shoghi Effendi, *God Passes By*, p. 75.
5. Bahá'u'lláh, *Epistle to the Son of the Wolf*, p. 14.
6. Ibid., p. 21.

Chapter 3: Solitude: Sojourn in Kurdistan

1. Bahá'u'lláh, *Bahá'í Prayers* (Wilmette: Bahá'í Publishing Trust, 1985) p. 214.
2. Bahá'u'lláh, *Kitáb-i-Íqán* (Wilmette: Bahá'í Publishing Trust, 1950) p. 251.
3. Shoghi Effend, *God Passes By*, p. 125.
4. Ibid., p. 135.
5. Bahá'u'lláh, *Hidden Words*, Arabic # 4, 22, 36, 55.
6. Bahá'u'lláh, *Kitáb-i-Aqdas*, (Haifa: Bahá'í World Center, 1992) p. 139.
7. Bahá'u'lláh, *Kitáb-i-Íqán*, p. 152.

Chapter 4: Paradise: The Garden of Ridvan

1. 'Abdu'l-Bahá, *Bahá'í Prayers*, p. 32.
2. Myron H. Phelps, *The Master in 'Akka* (Los Angeles: Kalimát Press, 1985) p. 48.
3. Bahá'u'lláh, *The Proclamation of Bahá'u'lláh* (Haifa: Bahá'í World Center, 1972) p. 11.
4. Ibid., p. 10.
5. Ibid., p. 12.
6. Bahá'u'lláh, *Gleanings from the Writings of Bahá'u'lláh* (Wilmette: Bahá'í Publishing Trust, 1939) pp. 250-251.

7. Shoghi Effendi, *The Promised Day is Come* (Wilmette: Bahá'í Publishing Trust, 1969) p. 65.
8. Adib Taherzadeh, *The Revelation of Bahá'u'lláh*, Volume II, p. 201.
9. Bahá'u'lláh, *Epistle to the Son of the Wolf*, p. 52.

Chapter 5: Final Exile: The Most Desolate of Cities

1. Bahá'u'lláh, *Gleanings*, p. 100.
2. Shoghi Effendi, *God Passes By*, pp. 179-80.
3. Ibid., p. 180.
4. Ibid., p. 182.
5. Phelps, *The Master in 'Akka*, p. 78.
6. Bahá'u'lláh, *The Summons of the Lord of Hosts* (Haifa: Bahá'í World Center, 2002) p. 156.
7. Ibid., p. 147.
8. Shoghi Effendi, *God Passes By*, p. 188.
9. Bahá'u'lláh, *Kitáb-i-Aqdas*, p. 19.
10. Ibid., p. 21.
11. Bahá'u'lláh, *Tablets*, p. 27.
12. Ibid., pp. 66-67.

Chapter 6: The Country: A Devotion Kings Might Envy

1. Quoted in Browne, *A Traveller's Narrative*, (Cambridge University Press, 1891) p. xl.
2. Balyuzi, *Bahá'u'lláh*, p. 357.
3. Ibid., pp. 358-359.
4. 'Abdu'l-Bahá, *Memorials of the Faithful*, p. 29.
5. Bahá'u'lláh, *Hidden Words*, Persian, # 51.
6. Bahá'u'lláh, *Tablets*, p. 105.
7. Bahá'u'lláh, *Hidden Words*, Arabic, # 64.
8. Bahá'u'lláh, *Epistle to the Son of the Wolf*, p. 99.
9. Ibid., p. 102.
10. E. G. Browne, *A Year Amongst the Persians* (Cambridge: University Press, 1927) p. 361.

Chapter 7: Final Passage: A Vision for the Ages

1. Bahá'u'lláh, *Gleanings*, p. 139.
2. Browne, *A Traveller's Narrative*, p. xxxiv-xl.
3. Taherzadeh, *Revelation*, Volume IV, p. 415.

Part Two: Bahá'í Principles

Chapter 8: Transition and Succession

1. Bahá'u'lláh, *Tablets*, p. 168.
2. Bahá'u'lláh, *Gleanings*, p. 286.
3. 'Abdu'l-Bahá, *The Promulgation of Universal Peace* (Wilmette: Bahá'í Publishing Trust, 1982) pp. 322-23.

Chapter 9: Social Principles

1. 'Abdu'l-Bahá, *Promulgation*, p. 322.
2. Bahá'u'lláh, *Gleanings*, p. 218.
3. 'Abdu'l-Bahá, *Promulgation*, p. 322.
4. Bahá'u'lláh, *Hidden Words*, Arabic, # 2.
5. 'Abdu'l-Bahá, *Selections from the Writings of 'Abdu'l-Baha* (Haifa: Bahá'í World Centre, 1978) p. 248.
6. 'Abdu'l-Bahá, *Promulgation*, p. 291.
7. Bahá'u'lláh, *Epistle to the Son of the Wolf*, p. 13.
8. 'Abdu'l-Bahá, *Paris Talks* (London: Bahá'í Publishing Trust, 1912) p. 130.
9. Bahá'u'lláh, *Tablets*, p. 162.
10. 'Abdu'l-Bahá, *Promulgation*, p. 300.
11. 'Abdu'l-Bahá, *Paris Talks*, pp. 130-31.
12. 'Abdu'l-Bahá, *Promulgation*, p. 316.
13. Bahá'u'lláh, *Women: Extracts from the Writings of Bahá'u'lláh, 'Abdu'l-Bahá, Shoghi Effendi and the Universal House of Justice* (Ontario: Bahá'í Canada Publications, 1986) p. 26.
14. 'Abdu'l, *Promulgation*, p. 174.

15. Ibid., p. 232.
16. Bahá'u'lláh, *Hidden Words*, Persian, # 82.
17. Ibid., # 49.
18. 'Abdu'l-Bahá, *Paris Talks*, p. 153.
19. Bahá'u'lláh, *Tablets*, p. 166.
20. 'Abdu'l-Bahá, *Promulgation*, pp. 232-33.
21. Ibid., p. 317.

Part Three: The Teachings of Bahá'u'lláh

Chapter 10: Our Spiritual Reality

1. J. E. Esslemont, *Bahá'u'lláh and the New Era* (Wilmette: Bahá'í Publishing Trust, 1980) p. 81.
2. Bahá'u'lláh, *Tablets*, p. 156.
3. *Genesis* 2:7, King James Version.
4. Bahá'u'lláh, *Gleanings*, p. 158.
5. Bahá'u'lláh, *Tablets*, p. 257.
6. Bahá'u'lláh, *Gleanings*, p. 261.
7. Bahá'u'lláh, *Tablets*, p. 257.

Chapter 11: Spiritual Virtues

1. Bahá'u'lláh, *Gleanings*, p. 196.
2. Bahá'u'lláh, *Hidden Words*, Arabic #4, 19, Persian, # 4.
3. Bahá'u'lláh, *Epistle to the Son of the Wolf*, pp. 93-94.
4. 'Abdu'l-Bahá, *Selections*, p. 202.
5. 'Abdu'l-Bahá, *Paris Talks*, p. 175.
6. Bahá'u'lláh, *Epistle to the Son of the Wolf*, p. 28.
7. 'Abdu'l-Bahá, *Selections*, p. 118.
8. Ibid., p. 125.
9. 'Abdu'l-Bahá, *Promulgation*, pp. 144-145.
10. Ibid., p. 168.
11. Ibid., p. 15.
12. 'Abdu'l-Bahá, *Promulgation*, p. 27.

13. Bahá'u'lláh, *Epistle to the Son of the Wolf*, p. 50.
14. 'Abdu'l-Bahá, *Selections*, p. 34.
15. Esslemont, *Bahá'u'lláh*, p. 81.
16. Bahá'u'lláh, *Hidden Words*, Arabic #1.
17. Bahá'u'lláh, *Gleanings*, p. 215.
18. Bahá'u'lláh, *Hidden Words*, Arabic #27, 29.
19. Esslemont, *Bahá'u'lláh*, p. 83.
20. Bahá'u'lláh, *Kitáb-i-Íqán*, p. 194.
21. Esslemont, *Bahá'u'lláh*, pp. 81-82.
22. 'Abdu'l-Bahá, *Some Answered Questions* (Wilmette: Bahá'í Publishing Trust, 1981) p. 269.
23. Bahá'u'lláh, *Gleanings*, p. 278.
24. Bahá'u'lláh, *Hidden Words*, Arabic #2.
25. Bahá'u'lláh, *Tablets*, p. 37.
26. Bahá'u'lláh, *Gleanings*, p. 297.
27. Ibid., p. 250.
28. 'Abdu'l-Bahá, *Paris Talks*, pp. 176-77.

Chapter 12: The True Seeker

1. Bahá'u'lláh, *The Seven Valleys and the Four Valleys* (Wilmette: Bahá'í Publishing Trust, 1991) p. 7.
2. Bahá'u'lláh, *Gleanings*, pp. 264-267.
3. Bahá'u'lláh, *Hidden Words*, Persian #52.
4. Bahá'u'lláh, *Tablets*, p. 16.
5. Bahá'u'lláh, *Gleanings*, pp. 96-97.
6. 'Abdu'l-Bahá, *Promulgation*, p. 100.

Chapter 13: Your Spiritual Path

1. Bahá'u'lláh, *Prayers and Meditations*, p. 248.
2. Bahá'u'lláh, *Hidden Words*, Persian #37, 70.
3. Ibid., #9.
4. Bahá'u'lláh, *Prayers and Meditations*, p. 250.
5. Ibid., pp. 264-265.
6. 'Abdu'l-Bahá, *Bahá'í Prayers*, pp. 71-72.

Suggested Reading

Some other books about Baha'u'llah:

H. M. Balyuzi. *Bahá'u'lláh: The King of Glory*. Oxford: George Ronald, 1980.
   A full biography of the founder of the Baha'i Faith.
J. E. Esslemont. *Bahá'u'lláh and the New Era*. Fifth Revised Edition. Wilmette, Ill.: Bahá'í Publishing Trust, 1980.
   A general introduction to Baha'i history and teachings.
Mary Perkins. *Days of Glory: The Life of Bahá'u'lláh*. Oxford: George Ronald, 1992.
   A short and readable book.
David S. Ruhe. *Robe of Light: The Persian Years of the Supreme Prophet Bahá'u'lláh, 1817-1853*. Oxford: George Ronald, 1994.
   The story of the early life of Baha'u'llah.
Ustad Muhammad-'Alíy-i Salmání. *My Memories of Bahá'u'lláh*. Trans. by Marziel Gail. Los Angeles: Kalimát Press, 1982.
   The memoir of one of Baha'u'llah's companions in exile.
Tarázu'lláh Samandarí. *Moments with Bahá'u'lláh: Memoirs of the Hand of the Cause of God Tarázu'lláh Samandarí*. Los Angeles: Kalimát Press, 1995.
   Glimpses of Baha'u'llah's later years.

Some books about 'Abdu'l-Baha:

H. M. Balyuzi. *'Abdu'l-Bahá: The Center of the Covenant of Bahá'u'lláh*. Oxford: George Ronald, 1971. A full biography.

Myron Phelps. *The Master in 'Akká*. Los Angeles: Kalimát Press, 1985 (1903).
   A readable introduction to Baha'i history and 'Abdu'l-Baha's ministry.

Steven Scholl, ed. *The Wisdom of the Master: The Spiritual Teachings of 'Abdu'l-Bahá*. Los Angeles: Kalimát Press, 1997.
   Stories about and quotations from 'Abdu'l-Baha.

◆

Baha'i websites:

www.bahai.org.
A comprehensive introduction to the Baha'i Faith

www.bahai.com/thebahais/
On-line version of *The Baha'is* magazine

www.bahaibooksonline.com
A comprehensive source for Baha'i books, music, and more, from a variety of publishers

www.bahaiworldnews.org
Baha'i World News

www.kalimat.com
Books from Kalimát Press

www.us.bahai.org
The official site of the Baha'is of the United States

To find a Baha'i community near you, call:

1-800-22-UNITE (228-6483)

We welcome your friendship whether or not you decide to become a Baha'i.